Bloom's BioCritiques

Dante Alighieri
Maya Angelou
Jane Austen
The Brontë Sisters
Lord Byron
Albert Camus
Geoffrey Chaucer
Anton Chekhov
Joseph Conrad
Stephen Crane
Charles Dickens
Emily Dickinson
T. S. Eliot
Ralph Ellison
William Faulkner
F. Scott Fitzgerald
Robert Frost
Nathaniel Hawthorne
Ernest Hemingway
Langston Hughes
Zora Neale Hurston
James Joyce
Stephen King
Arthur Miller
John Milton
Toni Morrison
Edgar Allan Poe
J. D. Salinger
William Shakespeare
John Steinbeck
Henry David Thoreau
Mark Twain
Alice Walker
Walt Whitman
Tennessee Williams
William Wordsworth

Bloom's BioCritiques

RALPH ELLISON

Edited and with an introduction by
Harold Bloom
Sterling Professor of the Humanities
Yale University

CHELSEA HOUSE
PUBLISHERS
A Haights Cross Communications Company
Philadelphia

10 9 8 7 6 5 4 3 2 1

Library of Congress Cataloging-in-Publication Data

Ralph Ellison / edited and with an introduction by Harold Bloom.
        p. cm. -- (Bloom's biocritiques)
Includes bibliographical references and index.
    ISBN 0-7910-6374-7
  1. Ellison, Ralph--Criticism and interpretation. 2. African
Americans in literature. I. Bloom, Harold. II. Series.
    PS3555.L625Z87 2003
    818'.5409--dc21

                                        2003001602

Chelsea House Publishers
1974 Sproul Road, Suite 400
Broomall, PA 19008-0914

http://www.chelseahouse.com

Contributing editor: Thomas Heise

Cover design by Keith Trego

Cover: © Bettman/CORBIS

Layout by EJB Publishing Services

CONTENTS

User's Guide

These volumes are designed to introduce the reader to the life and work of the world's literary masters. Each volume begins with Harold Bloom's essay "The Work in the Writer" and a volume-specific introduction also written by Professor Bloom. Following these unique introductions is an engaging biography that discusses the major life events and important literary accomplishments of the author under consideration.

Furthermore, each volume includes an original critique that not only traces the themes, symbols, and ideas apparent in the author's works, but strives to put those works into a cultural and historical perspective. In addition to the original critique is a brief selection of significant critical essays previously published on the author and his or her works followed by a concise and informative chronology of the writer's life. Finally, each volume concludes with a bibliography of the writer's works, a list of additional readings, and an index of important themes and ideas.

HAROLD BLOOM

The Work in the Writer

Literary biography found its masterpiece in James Boswell's *Life of Samuel Johnson*. Boswell, when he treated Johnson's writings, implicitly commented upon Johnson as found in his work, even as in the great critic's life. Modern instances of literary biography, such as Richard Ellmann's lives of W. B. Yeats, James Joyce, and Oscar Wilde, essentially follow in Boswell's pattern.

That the writer somehow is in the work, we need not doubt, though with William Shakespeare, writer-of-writers, we almost always need to rely upon pure surmise. The exquisite rancidities of the Problem Plays or Dark Comedies seem to express an extraordinary estrangement of Shakespeare from himself. When we read or attend *Troilus and Cressida* and *Measure for Measure*, we may be startled by particular speeches of Ulysses in the first play, or of Vincentio in the second. These speeches, of Ulysses upon hierarchy or upon time, or of Duke Vincentio upon death, are too strong either for their contexts or for the characters of their speakers. The same phenomenon occurs with Parolles, the military impostor of *All's Well That Ends Well*. Utterly disgraced, he nevertheless affirms: "Simply the thing I am/Shall make me live."

In Shakespeare, more even than in his peers, Dante and Cervantes, meaning always starts itself again through excess or overflow. The strongest of Shakespeare's creatures—Falstaff, Hamlet, Iago, Lear, Cleopatra—have an exuberance that is fiercer than their plays can contain. If Ben Jonson was at all correct in his complaint that "Shakespeare wanted art," it could have been only in a sense that he may not have intended. Where do the personalities of Falstaff or Hamlet touch a limit? What was it in Shakespeare that made the two parts of *Henry IV* and *Hamlet* into "plays unlimited"? Neither Falstaff nor Hamlet will be stopped: their wit, their beautiful, laughing speech, their intensity of being—all these are virtually infinite.

In what ways do Falstaff and Hamlet manifest the writer in the work? Evidently, we can never know, or know enough to answer with any authority. But what would happen if we reversed the question, and asked: How did the work form the writer, Shakespeare?

Of Shakespeare's inwardness, his biography tells us nothing. And yet, to an astonishing extent, Shakespeare created our inwardness. At the least, we can speculate that Shakespeare so lived his life as to conceal the depths of his nature, particularly as he rather prematurely aged. We do not have Shakespeare on Shakespeare, as any good reader of the Sonnets comes to realize: they do not constitute a key that unlocks his heart. No sequence of sonnets could be less confessional or more powerfully detached from the poet's self.

The German poet and universal genius, Goethe, affords a superb contrast to Shakespeare. Of Goethe's life, we know more than everything; I wonder sometimes if we know as much about Napoleon or Freud or any other human being who ever has lived, as we know about Goethe. Everywhere, we can find Goethe in his work, so much so that Goethe seems to crowd the writing out, just as Byron and Oscar Wilde seem to usurp their own literary accomplishments. Goethe, cunning beyond measure, nevertheless invested a rival exuberance in his greatest works that could match his personal charisma. The sublime outrageousness of the Second Part of *Faust*, or of the greater lyric and meditative poems, form a Counter-Sublime to Goethe's own daemonic intensity.

Goethe was fascinated by the daemonic in himself; we can doubt that Shakespeare had any such interests. Evidently, Shakespeare abandoned his acting career just before he composed *Measure for Measure* and *Othello*. I surmise that the egregious interventions by Vincentio and Iago displace the actor's energies into a new kind of mischief-making, a fresh opening to a subtler playwriting-within-the-play.

But what had opened Shakespeare to this new awareness? The answer is the work in the writer, *Hamlet* in Shakespeare. One can go further: it was not so much the play, *Hamlet*, as the character Hamlet, who changed Shakespeare's art forever.

Hamlet's personality is so large and varied that it rivals Goethe's own. Ironically Goethe's Faust, his Hamlet, has no personality at all, and is as colorless as Shakespeare himself seems to have chosen to be. Yet nothing could be more colorful than the Second Part of *Faust*, which is peopled by an astonishing array of monsters, grotesque devils, and classical ghosts.

A contrast between Shakespeare and Goethe demonstrates that in each—but in very different ways—we can better find the work in the person, than we can discover that banal entity, the person in the work. Goethe to many of his contemporaries, seemed to be a mortal god. Shakespeare, so far as we know, seemed an affable, rather ordinary fellow, who aged early and became somewhat withdrawn. Yet Faust, though Mephistopheles battles for his soul, is hardly worth the trouble unless you take him as an idea and not as a person. Hamlet is nearly every-idea-in-one, but he is precisely a personality and a person.

Would Hamlet be so astonishingly persuasive if his father's ghost did not haunt him? Falstaff is more alive than Prince Hal, who says that the devil haunts him in the shape of an old fat man. Three years before composing the final *Hamlet*, Shakespeare invented Falstaff, who then never ceased to haunt his creator. Falstaff and Hamlet may be said to best represent the work in the writer, because their influence upon Shakespeare was prodigious. W.H. Auden accurately observed that Falstaff possesses infinite energy: never tired, never bored, and absolutely both witty and happy until Hal's rejection destroys him. Hamlet too has infinite energy, but in him it is more curse than blessing.

Falstaff and Hamlet can be said to occupy the roles in Shakespeare's invented world that Sancho Panza and Don Quixote possess in Cervantes's. Shakespeare's plays from 1610 on (starting with *Twelfth Night*) are thus analogous to the Second Part of Cervantes's epic novel. Sancho and the Don overtly jostle Cervantes for authorship in the Second Part, even as Cervantes battles against the impostor who has pirated a continuation of his work. As a dramatist, Shakespeare manifests the work in the writer more indirectly. Falstaff's prose genius is revived in the scapegoating of Malvolio by Maria and Sir Toby Belch, while Falstaff's darker insights are developed by Feste's melancholic wit. Hamlet's intellectual resourcefulness, already deadly, becomes poisonous in Iago and in Edmund. Yet we have not crossed into the deeper abysses of the work in the writer in later Shakespeare.

No fictive character, before or since, is Falstaff's equal in self-trust. Sir John, whose delight in himself is contagious, has total confidence both in his self-awareness and in the resources of his language. Hamlet, whose self is as strong, and whose language is as copious, nevertheless distrusts both the self and language. Later Shakespeare is, as it were, much under the influence both of Falstaff and of Hamlet, but they tug him in opposite directions. Shakespeare's own copiousness of language is well-nigh incredible: a vocabulary in excess of twenty-one thousand words, almost eighteen hundred of which he coined himself. And of his word-hoard, nearly half are used only once each, as though the perfect setting for each had been found, and need not be repeated. Love for language and faith in language are Falstaffian attributes. Hamlet will darken both that love and that faith in Shakespeare, and perhaps the Sonnets can best be read as Falstaff and Hamlet counterpointing against one another.

Can we surmise how aware Shakespeare was of Falstaff and Hamlet, once they had played themselves into existence? *Henry IV, Part I* appeared in six quarto editions during Shakespeare's lifetime; *Hamlet* possibly had four. Falstaff and Hamlet were played again and again at the Globe, but Shakespeare knew also that they were being read, and he must have had contact with some of those readers. What would it have been like to discuss Falstaff or Hamlet with one of their early readers (presumably also part of their audience at the Globe), if you were the creator of such demiurges? The question would seem nonsensical to most Shakespeare scholars, but then these days they tend to be either ideologues or moldy figs. How can we recover the uncanniness of Falstaff and of Hamlet, when they now have become so familiar?

A writer's influence upon himself is an unexplored problem in criticism, but such an influence is never free from anxieties. The biocritical problem (which this series attempts to explore) can be divided into two areas, difficult to disengage fully. Accomplished works affect the author's life, and also affect her subsequent writings. It is simpler for me to surmise the effect of *Mrs. Dalloway* and *To the Lighthouse* upon Woolf's late *Between the Acts*, than it is to relate Clarissa Dalloway's suicide and Lily Briscoe's capable endurance in art to the tragic death and complex life of Virginia Woolf.

There are writers whose lives were so vivid that they seem sometimes to obscure the literary achievement: Byron, Wilde, Malraux, Hemingway. But most major Western writers do not live that exuberantly, and the greatest of all, Shakespeare, sometimes appears to have adopted the personal mask of colorlessness. And yet there are heroes of literature who struggled titanically with their own eras— Tolstoy, Milton, Victor Hugo—who nevertheless matter more for their works than their lives.

There are great figures—Emily Dickinson, Wallace Stevens, Willa Cather—who seem to have had so little of the full intensity of life when compared to the vitality of their work, that we might almost speak of the work in the work, rather than even of the work in a person. Emily Brontë might well be the extreme instance of such a visionary, surpassing William Blake in that one regard.

I conclude this general introduction to a series of literary bio-critiques by stating a tentative formula or principle for gauging the many ways in which the work influences the person and her subsequent, later work. Our influence upon ourselves is always related to the Shakespearean invention of self-overhearing, which I have written about in several other contexts. Life, as well as poetry and prose, is overheard rather than simply heard. The writer listens to herself as though she were somebody else, and the will to change begins to operate. The forces that live in us include the prior work we have done, and the dreams and waking visions that evade our dismissals.

HAROLD BLOOM

Introduction

The influence of *Invisible Man* (1952) upon the forty-two years remaining to Ralph Ellison (1914-1994) was prodigious, surmounting the effect of *Leaves of Grass* (1855) upon Walt Whitman (1819-1892). The posthumously published "second novel," *Juneteenth*, was put together by his editors, and adds very little to the lasting glory of *Invisible Man*. In the half-century since first I read Ellison's masterwork, I have reread it six or seven times, and probably could reproduce verbally much if not most of it by memory. Over the forty years or so in which I enjoyed conversations with Ellison, mostly in New York City, I found myself charting involuntarily something of the fortunes of the work in his life.

Ralph Waldo Ellison's long, stubborn resistance to being subsumed by the lemmings of resentment began with his refusal, in 1965, to participate in a conference of "black writers" at the New School for Social Research. For the three decades following, he maintained his individualistic stance. I remember Elizabeth Bishop declining, more than once, to having her poems anthologized in volumes devoted entirely to "women poets." One didn't see Charlie Parker push Red Rodney off the bandstand, or Lester Young decline to perform with Gerry Mulligan. Great artists resist recruitment by ideologies founded upon ethnicity, race, gender, sexual orientation, and all the other means tests that have debilitated our institutions of "higher" education. I will not say of "learning," because it is decades now since I have heard a professor or a student commended for learning.

I think the bad time that started in the mid-sixties and continues unabated early in the new century had much to do with Ralph Ellison's endless delays in composing a second major narrative. And yet the primary element in his creative impasse was intrinsic: the aesthetic eminence of *Invisible Man*, one of the principal American novels since William Faulkner's great sequence of *The Sound and the Fury*, *As I Lay Dying*, *Sanctuary*, *Light in August*, and *Absalom, Absalom!*, published from 1929 to 1936. *Invisible Man* has only a few rivals in the agon to join that company: Nathanael West, Flannery O'Connor, Thomas Pynchon, Cormac McCarthy, Philip Roth, Don DeLillo. I might nominate *Miss Lonelyhearts*, *The Violent Bear It Away*, *Mason & Dixon*, *Blood Meridian*, *Sabbath's Theater*, and *Underworld* as the half-dozen books I would place on a shelf next to the major novels of William Faulkner and Willa Cather, and *Invisible Man*. These are the best the nation has accomplished since the death of Henry James.

Ellison found his literary precursors in Faulkner and Dostoevsky, and acknowledged debts also to Malraux and Hemingway. He omitted *Moby-Dick*, the palpable forerunner to *Invisible Man*, though Ellison's nameless protagonist is no Ahab. It has been argued cogently, by Bernt Ostendorf in particular, that Ellison's aesthetic stems more from the great masters of jazz, Louis Armstrong and Charlie Parker, than from such modernists as James Joyce and T. S. Eliot. Ellison's sense of the agonistic emanates from the jazz artist's "cutting contests":

> For true jazz is an art of individual assertion within and against the group. Each true jazz moment (as distinct from the uninspired commercial performance) springs from a context in which each artist challenges all the rest; each solo flight, or improvisation, represents (like the successive canvases of a painter) a definition of his identity: as individual, as member of the collectivity and as a link in the chain of tradition.

Ellison's "cutting contest" certainly involved Faulkner, and Dostoevsky's *Notes from Underground*, but *Invisible Man* emphasizes the Jonah motif, as Douglas Robinson first emphasizes. This is the Book of Jonah mediated by Father Mapple's sermon in *Moby-Dick*, and by the ultimate fate of Ishmael, in Melville's epic. *Invisible Man* is the new Jonah, and so was Ishmael: they survived to tell the story of all our catastrophes. Survivalism, rather than apocalypse, is the pragmatic prophecy of the American Jonah, Melville's Ishmael and Ellison's Invisible Man. Beyond all the recognition that he rightly received, Ellison was haunted by the freshness he had brought to the vision of Jonah. The sense of testifying to American survivalism, black *and* white, was a great burden for Ralph Waldo Ellison, whose life—as much as Proust's, Joyce's, Faulkner's—testified to the Work in the Writer.

NORMA JEAN LUTZ

Biography of Ralph Ellison

BACK TO THE TERRITORY

On a warm June evening in 1975, a celebration was in full swing at a home located in the northeast part of Oklahoma City, Oklahoma. Partygoers filled the house, spilling out onto the moonlit back lawn, talking, laughing and sharing old memories. The group consisted of graduates from the classes of 1931 and 1932 from the all-black, now-defunct Douglass High School. While the gathering appeared to be a typical class reunion, this group had assembled for a greater purpose than to simply reminisce; the reunion was being held in honor of the noted author Ralph W. Ellison. A new branch library had been named the Ralph Ellison Public Library in honor of the Oklahoma City native, and Ellison and his wife Fanny were in town for the dedication ceremony.

A classmate of Ellison's, James Stewart, had organized the reunion to coincide with the dedication, and had offered his home as the site for the commencement party. This location was a far cry from the neighborhood on Second Street—known in the thirties as Deep Second or Deep Deuce—where Stewart and Ellison had grown up together. Neither man could have imagined, as barefoot boys running about the neighborhood, that they would attain such levels of notoriety.

Stories and jokes were exchanged throughout the room as the alumni, who'd flown in from many different parts of the country, shared memories of days spent in the halls of Douglass High School, named for the black orator and abolitionist, Frederick Douglass.

Despite graduating from high school at a time when the United States was sinking into the Great Depression, many of Ellison's classmates had succeeded; their ranks contained teachers, school principals, superintendents, business owners, and one classmate had just become the first black municipal judge in the history of Oklahoma City. The host of the party, James Stewart, was an administrative officer of the Oklahoma Natural Gas Company, served on the city's Urban Renewal Authority, and was a member of the board of directors for the National Association for the Advancement of Colored People. In fact, one attendee was overheard to say that Stewart was "the man you go to whenever you want to find out what's going on in town." (Anderson, 4) These were Ellison's people; they represented his roots and he felt deeply indebted to them. He was to find a unique opportunity of telling them so the next morning.

A morning brunch was held at the University of Oklahoma's Faculty House and was attended by most of the guests from the previous evening with the addition of a few dignitaries. The mayor of Oklahoma City, Patience Latting, noted that Ralph Ellison was "a distinguished American, a gentleman whom Oklahoma City honors as a son by naming a library for him." (Anderson, 19)

Before leaving for the library dedication, the group asked Ellison to say a few words. Reluctantly, he stood and addressed them with a tremor in his voice "... there's no way for me to convey to you how important it is to see all your faces again—old friends, old antagonists, old teammates, old scapegoats and scapegoaters. I know that there are some among us who took off to explore the wider world during the Depression. We were taking chances; we had no idea how it was going to turn out. But you all came through. And you inspire me. You affirm my sense of life. You are testimonies to the faith of your fathers and mothers—especially the mothers." (Anderson, 19)

It was a clear and sunny day as the guests gathered at the branch library for the dedication. The low-lying, split-level, sloping library structure located on Northeast Twenty-Third Street—one of eleven branch libraries in the city—stands on a tract of land that used to be fields and woodlands when Ellison was growing up, and he specifically recalled hunting his first rabbits in that same area.

Inside the library foyer stands a sculpture featuring two portrait studies of Ralph Ellison—one pensive and serious, the other lighthearted. In tribute to Ellison's lifelong love of music, a jazz band played some of the author's favorite tunes. Hundreds of guests—including scores of politicians and community leaders—crowded into the facility, and all of them clamored for recognition. Black State Representative, Hannah Atkins introduced Ellison as a person who has brought honor to Oklahoma and has "done us proud." (Anderson, 21) Ellison's deep love for books and for libraries made it especially fitting that it be a library named in his honor, as his acceptance speech bore witness. After giving credit to those who had helped him along the way, and eulogizing the historical era and place from which he had come, Ellison turned to the subject of libraries:

> I shall be ever awed by, and thankful for, the honor you've bestowed upon me today. And I have no doubt that within these walls other writers—black, white, Indian—will emerge. And, if so, it will be because the library is a place where a child or an adult can make a connection between the rich oral tradition which we have inherited from the past and the literary rendering of American experience that is to be found in the library ... What we have to worry about is the maintenance and enlargement of the library. It is no accident that Fascists despise and fear books. They burn libraries. Why? Because the library is a nexus of dreams. The library is a place where we are able to free ourselves from the limitations of today by becoming acquainted with what went on in the past—and thus project ourselves into the future. (Anderson, 21)

That evening, Ellison and his wife Fanny were guests of honor at a dance where the author demonstrated that he could still stomp and riff with the best of them—dances he had learned as a boy at a time when budding jazz musicians played their innovative melodies in and around Deep Second.

Before returning to New York City, where Ellison had made his home for 40 years, he expressed regret that his mother, who had died in 1937, was not alive to share this moment with him. "I have a great feeling of regret that some of the people who were most helpful to me, and had such faith in me when I was growing up, were not here ..." he said, referring mainly to his mother. (Anderson, 21)

Ida (Millsap) Ellison, daughter of slaves, would have been proud indeed of her son's accomplishments, especially of the impact he'd had on the world of literature.

Growing Up in Oklahoma

In 1834, the U.S. government enacted the Indian Intercourse Act, effectively setting aside a section of land for Native Americans. Prior to this date, the U.S. government had forcefully moved the Cherokee, Creek, Seminole, Choctaw, and Chickasaw tribes—later known collectively as the Five Civilized Tribes—to the area which is now present-day Oklahoma, and for many years it was to be known as Indian Territory. In 1854 the territory was further limited by the creation of the Kansas and Nebraska territories and eventually it was abolished altogether when Oklahoma became a state in 1907.

When the Indian tribes moved to the Territory, they took with them established systems of slavery; mixed-blood Indians, (the offspring of white traders and frontiersmen who married Indian women), were the principal slaveholders in the tribes, largely because their fathers had taught them the economics of slavery. Those mixed-blood Indians remained tribal members and became important middlemen between white settlers and Indian communities.

Many Cherokee depended on black slaves as a bridge to white society, and full-blood Indian slave owners relied on the blacks as English interpreters and translators.

By 1860, the five combined tribes owned more than nine thousand slaves. Some of the Indian slave owners were as harsh and cruel as the white slave masters, and Indians were often hired to catch runaway slaves—in fact, slave-catching was a lucrative occupation for some, especially the Chickasaws.

These slaves became the first of the black settlers in the Territory; however their number was small in comparison to the mass migration that took place during the late 1880s following the collapse of Reconstruction. Those blacks came to Indian Territory to escape the persecution that had been entrenched in the South by hundreds of years of slavery. Because Oklahoma had never been a slave state, and because it was open for settlement, a number of communities were formed made up entirely of blacks.

Between 1865 and 1915, at least 60 black towns were established in the Territory and more than 20 of them were in Oklahoma. With the combined support and assistance from the Five Civilized Tribes, freedmen from the South settled the all-black towns of Oklahoma. Most of the towns were established by African Americans for African Americans on land that was formerly held by one of the Five Civilized Tribes. Many of the blacks that migrated there looked upon Oklahoma as their promised land; to them, the wide-open spaces represented a place of hope, of freedom, and of opportunity.

African Americans fought to keep the Jim Crow laws out of the state, but the freedoms they enjoyed were slowly curtailed as more whites arrived—prejudices still intact. Soon forms of segregation and discrimination surfaced, much as they existed in the South but never with the same intensity. Relationships between the races in Oklahoma tended to be more fluid than in the South, which gave blacks a greater sense of achievement.

African Americans living in Oklahoma experienced freedom enough to aggressively stand up for what they felt was rightfully theirs. As Ralph Ellison would later explain, although Oklahoma was Jim Crow "you knew about the villainies of white people, yet in Oklahoma it was possible to realize that it was not a blanket thing.... We had some violence, there was fighting between Negro and white boys, but it was not too deeply fixed in the traditions or psychology of people." (Graham, 65)

Two years after Oklahoma gained statehood, a young man named Lewis Ellison, along with his wife, Ida, arrived in Oklahoma City. Lewis Ellison was the son of slave parents and grew up in Abbeville, South Carolina, where he learned the construction trade from his father and his uncles—all of whom had been builders during their slavery days and who later built railroad trestles for the Southern Railroad during the Reconstruction period.

For a time, Lewis served in the Army, fighting in Cuba during the Spanish-American War, and later in the Philippines. He also fought in the Boxer Rebellion in China. Upon his return home, he and a partner operated an ice cream parlor in Abbeville, and during that time he met and married Ida Millsap from White Oak, Georgia. Ida Milsap Ellison was also a child of freed slaves.

The couple moved to Chattanooga, Tennessee, where Lewis Ellison and his brother first operated a candy kitchen and later a restaurant. From there he found better pay in construction work. Upon hearing about the land that was being settled in Oklahoma, the Ellisons left Chattanooga and made their way to Oklahoma City where they settled in a rooming house owned by a man named J.D. Randolph. The Randolph family would later play an integral part in the lives of the Ellison family.

Blacks in Oklahoma City at first were scattered throughout the town, but as segregation slowly took over, they congregated in the area of Second Street where a close-knit community developed, including small shops, rooming houses, bars, funeral parlors, barbershops, hairdressing establishments, drugstores, shoeshine stands, movie houses, juke joints, and dance halls.

Lewis Ellison became the foreman of a construction crew working on some of the first steel-and-concrete structures in the city. In addition, he also sold ice and coal house-to-house, gaining many friends in both the black and the white neighborhoods.

On March 1, 1914, Ida gave birth to a son whom Lewis insisted they name Ralph Waldo, after the famous New England poet, Ralph Waldo Emerson. The choice of name may have been due to Lewis's love of reading; or perhaps it was due to his appreciation for Emerson's works. Unfortunately, Ellison was never able to ask his father about his name; when Ralph was three and his baby brother Herbert was barely four months old, Lewis was killed in an accident.

Though he was only three when his father died, Ellison could remember a few things about Lewis, such as being taught to dance by him; at age two he could do the Eagle Rock and the Black Bottom, popular dances at that time among African Americans. He also remembered a song taught to him by his father which contained the phrase "I'm dark-brown chocolate to the bone," (Anderson, 13) and he had another memory of his father playing drums during a rehearsal at their neighborhood African Methodist Episcopal church.

Lewis Ellison had been a good father and an adequate provider; his loss placed extreme pressure and hardship upon Ida Ellison, who was now soley responsible for rearing her two sons. She never re-married and devoted the rest of her life to creating a good home environment for her two young sons.

A year after Lewis died, Ida found employment as janitor of the Avery Chapel Church. Because the minister owned a home, the church parsonage became available for Ida and her children to move into, and they lived there for over three years. Rent-free housing was only one of the benefits of the arrangement; Ellison always clearly remembered the shelves full of books that had been left in the house, and how at an early age he began to read the novels stored there. He was a voracious reader, having read James Fenimore Cooper's *The Last of the Mohicans* ten times by the time he was eight years old.

Later Ida found work cleaning houses for the wealthy, white families in the city, and she brought home discarded books and copies of magazines such as *Vanity Fair* and *Literary Digest*, as well as opera recordings. As he perused these materials, Ellison caught a glimpse of a larger world outside his own, and rather than considering them unattainable, he saw them as "things which spoke of a world which I could some day make my own." (Ellison, *Shadow*, 5)

Ida had great aspirations for her two sons, and instead of purchasing ordinary toys, she bought things like a phonograph and records, electrical sets and chemical sets—items to challenge and stimulate their imaginations and creativity. Ellison remembered one special Christmas when he was barely five, his gifts consisted of a small roll-top desk and a chair, complete with a toy typewriter. Ida worked hard to provide life's necessities, and she always made sure her sons' minds were challenged.

The J.D. Randolph family, neighbors of the Ellisons, helped to care for the boys while Ida was away at work. One morning it was bitterly cold and snowing, and the Randolphs were sure Brownie (Ida's nickname in the community) would never try to make it to work, but Mrs. Randolph decided she had better go and check on the boys just to be safe. Sure enough, Ida had gone to work, the fire had gone out, and the two boys were huddled together trying to keep warm.

As an adult, the Randolph's son Taylor would recall that wintry day. "My mother took them right back to our house and kept them there until Brownie came home from work. This was a time when there was a great togetherness among families, and when there was a great sympathy for people who had to struggle to bring up their children." (Anderson, 15)

As a boy in grammar school, Ellison struggled beneath the weight of his powerful literary name, which puzzled him because he knew nothing about poets or poetry; he often wondered why he hadn't been named for a famous war hero, or an educator like Booker T. Washington. Or, better yet, why hadn't his father—like so many black parents during that era—named him after President Theodore Roosevelt?

While Ellison was still too small to understand, adults would tease and call him "Ralph Waldo Emerson," which caused him no end of consternation, and he would answer, "No, *no*, I'm not Emerson; he's the little boy who lives next door." It would be many years before he fully grasped the significance of the poet for whom he was named. "Much later, after I began to write and work with words, I came to suspect that he (Lewis Ellison) was aware of the suggestive powers of names and of the magic involved in naming ..." (Anderson, 13) As an adult, he happened to meet one of his cousins who told him that his father used to say, "I'm raising this boy to be a poet." (Graham, 273)

By the time he reached the age when Emerson's works were studied in the classroom, Ellison had stopped using Waldo altogether and substituted it with the initial "W," and in his own reading avoided the poet's works like the plague. At an early age, Ellison loved to tinker and build things, especially electrical equipment. He was fascinated with building radios—both crystal sets and circuits—and he learned those building methods by reading the popular radio magazines of the twenties. Most amateur radio builders used cylindrical ice-cream cartons to wind the tuning coils, and the best place to find the cartons was in the trash. When Ellison was about eight-years-old, while he was searching through the trash for cartons, he met a white boy who was looking for the same items. (At that time in his life, the Ellisons were living in a white middle-class neighborhood where Ida managed an apartment house.)

Ellison and the white boy, whose nickname was Hoolie, became instant friends. Hoolie was tutored at home because of a heart condition and his mother was pleased that her son had a new friend. As he was the only black child in a white neighborhood, Ellison too was lonely.

Hoolie had become adept at taking apart his family's large radio and putting it back together again, and the two boys spent hours working on electronic experiments together. By the time Ellison's mother moved the family back to Deep Second, Hoolie was ready to apply for his ham radio license. Ellison was to look back at the friendship as a meaningful one in his life—and not because of the issue of race. "It was important for me to know a boy who could approach the intricacies of electronics with such daring and whose mind was intellectually aggressive. Knowing him led me to expect much more of myself and of the world." (*Shadow*, 5)

Music became a vitalizing factor throughout Ellison's childhood years and helped to shape his life in a number of ways. In the black neighborhood where he grew up, music was omnipresent and affected everyone. In the home of his cousins, his aunt might be singing hymns to the accompaniment of the player piano, upon which, at another time, one of the cousins might be plunking out the melody of "Squeeze Me." Among the people of the neighborhood were self-taught musicians "playing guitars, Jew's harps, kazoos, yukes, mandolins, C Melody saxophones, or performed on combs by vibrating a piece of tissue paper placed against the comb's teeth. Much of this was improvised music, including blues and jazz riffs." (Graham, 303) To his young ears came the songs of the watermelon men with "voices like mellow bugles" who "shouted their wares in time with the rhythm of their horses' hoofs" and the washerwomen singing "slave songs as they stirred sooty tubs in sunny yards ...". (Ellison *Shadow*, 197)

Not only was there good quality and quantity of music, but there was also a wide variety—military and concert bands, jazz orchestras and gig combos, standard marches used in the school band, and formal religious music at church. And added to the list was an appreciation of the classics, which were taught in the schools.

A neighbor, Mr. Mead, taught Ralph the fundamentals of playing the brass alto horn and Ida was able to purchase for him a pawnshop cornet. To Ralph, having his own instrument meant he could spend more hours practicing, and he was accepted into the school band at the age of eight.

In the school band, Ellison related, "we played military music, the classic marches, arrangements of symphonic music, overtures, snatches of opera ... and we sang classical sacred music and the Negro spirituals." (*Shadow*, 11) Students were taught four years of harmony and two years of musical form, which was rare for the schools of the day, be they white or black. The richer, deeper jazz experiences, of which Ellison would later write extensively, came later during his high school years.

Distinctive black folklore was to provide yet another thread in the tapestry of a childhood woven on Deep Second Street; it was part of the talk at the barbershops, and the other shops and stores. During cotton-picking season some of Ellison's classmates would leave school to go work in the cotton fields with their parents, and while he did not remember them talking about the hard work, they came home with new black jokes and stories, which Ellison had never heard before; through this he sensed the richness of his own heritage and background.

The formative years for Ralph Ellison were secure and most of his memories were good ones, despite the fact that Deep Second bore the nickname of the Bloody Bucket. "A lot of cutting and shooting went on, especially on Friday and Saturday nights." (Anderson, 15) Fortunately, and undoubtedly due to Ida Ellison's diligence in child-rearing, Ralph Ellison escaped the violence that was such a common occurrence.

BECOMING A RENAISSANCE MAN

The four years Ellison spent at all-black Douglass High School—from 1929 to 1933—were busy ones. In order to help with household expenses he held a number of odd jobs, which included mowing lawns, hawking newspapers, working as an elevator operator, shining shoes, and jerking sodas at the Randolph's Drug Store. At the same time, he continued his study of music, wearing out the neighbors' ears and sensibilities with daily horn practice next to his open bedroom window:

> Indeed, I terrorized a good part of an entire city section. During summer vacation I blew sustained tones out of the window for hours, usually starting—especially on Sunday mornings—before breakfast. I sputtered whole days through M. Arban's (he's the great authority on the instrument) double- and triple-tonguing exercises—with an effect like that of a jackass hiccupping off a big meal of briars. During school-term mornings I practiced a truly exhibitionist "Reveille" before leaving for school, and in the evening I generously gave the ever-listening world a long, slow version of "Taps," ineptly played but throbbing with what in my adolescent vagueness felt was a romantic sadness. (*Shadow*, 191)

Along with several high school friends, Ellison dreamed of being a latter-day "Renaissance man," and that meant striving for excellence in every aspect of life. The hard work that was required to reach his dream never fazed Ellison, for he was highly disciplined. He wanted nothing to pass him by, and he wanted to soak up the sights, sounds, stories, yarns, tales, myths, and culture that surrounded him—from the blacks, the whites, and the Native Americans.

When looking back at his childhood memories he described the "Indian-Negro confusion," with tongue-in-cheek humor. "There were Negroes who were part Indian and who lived on reservations, and Indians who had children who lived in town as Negroes, and Negroes who were Indians and traveled back and forth between the groups with no trouble. And Indians who were as wild as wild Negroes and others who were as solid and as steady as bankers." (Ellison *Shadow*, 159)

Ellison worked hard to excel; hence he wasn't always the most popular boy in school. His friend James Stewart remembered that Ellison was "bright and he was studious, but he had a sharp tongue.... He made the rest of us uncomfortable, probably because he knew we weren't as bright as he was, and because he didn't let us forget it.... He was a director of the high-school band, and he played tackle on the football team." (Anderson, 4)

That he was fatherless caused Ellison very little difficulty in his life since the close-knit community provided him with a number of father substitutes. One such person was J.D. Randolph in whose boardinghouse Ralph had been born.

J.D. (named for Jefferson Davis) Randolph had been one of the leaders of a group of blacks who walked from Gallatin, Tennessee, to the Oklahoma Territory; upon his arrival in Oklahoma City in 1889, he founded a school for the black children living there. That same school became Douglass High School, the first high school for blacks in the city.

Randolph became like an adopted grandfather to Ellison during his childhood and Ellison remembered the older man as "a tall man, as brown as smoked leather, who looked like the Indians with whom he'd herded horses in the early days." (Ellison *Shadow*, 156)

In 1903, Randolph's daughter Edna married Dr. W.H. Slaughter, who was the only black doctor in the area. The Slaughter Building (Slaughter's Hall as it was known) located on the corner of Second Street and Stiles Avenue, housed the first black library, created from a couple of rooms lined with shelves and filled with books. J.D. Randolph opened a drugstore on the first floor, and his sons Taylor and James helped him run the business.

Randolph held a part-time job working as custodian in the law library of the Oklahoma State Capitol, and young Ellison often accompanied him and worked alongside him as he swept and cleaned. Ellison would recall white legislators coming into the law library and questioning Randolph on points of law. "... Often I was to hear him answer without recourse to the uniform rows of books on the shelves," Ellison recalled. "This was a thing to marvel at in itself, and the white lawmakers did so, but even more marvelous ... is the fact that the Negro who knew the answers was named after Jefferson Davis. What Tennessee lost, Oklahoma was to gain, and after gaining it (a gift of courage, intelligence, fortitude and grace), used it only in concealment and one hopes, with embarrassment." (Ellison *Shadow*, 156)

Ellison had a job selling newspapers, which brought him into contact with Roscoe Dunjee, editor of the local *Black Dispatch*. Although at the time he had little interest in writing, Dunjee's courage and dedication would affect him in later years. Dunjee always stressed political issues and was unafraid to initiate editorial controversy with writers and editors of the *Daily Oklahoma* and the *Oklahoma City Times*. "He had a tremendous impact," Ellison said, "because he was very articulate and a number of white people read what he had to say." (Graham, 258)

Another man who was to exert a strong influence in Ellison's life was Ludwig Hebestreit, the white conductor of the Oklahoma City Orchestra and band director at the segregated Classen High School. In exchange for mowing the conductor's lawn, Ralph received private music lessons on his trumpet and Hebestreit treated his young student with utmost respect. The lessons would extend far past the allotted time as the conductor talked endlessly about the lives of his favorite composers, Beethoven, Wagner and Schumann and expanded into the technical aspects of symphonic structure:

> Most of it was over my head, but he made it all so logical, and better still, he taught me how to attack those things I desired so that I could pierce the mystery and possess them. I came to feel, yes, that if you want these things and master

the technique, you could get with it. You could make it yours. (*Shadow*, 13)

The sessions increased Ellison's knowledge of classical music and prompted both a desire to write symphonies and the belief that he could do it. Interaction with Hebestreit and other members of the white community also built within Ralph a respect and trust of whites.

Mrs. Zelia N. Breaux was Ellison's music teacher at Douglass and provided advanced training in music using a variety of outlets including marching and concert band, glee clubs, an orchestra and chorus, and an annual operetta performed by students. Mrs. Breaux, whose father was the school principal, Dr. Inman Page, did not encourage her pupils to play jazz; however, she did bring jazz musicians to the Aldridge Theater which she managed, and names like King Oliver, Ma Rainey, Ida Cox and Bessie Smith were often on the bill.

Jazz groups gathered to play and conducted jam sessions in a large room on the top floor of Slaughter's Hall, and also in Hallie Richardson's Shoe Shine Parlor. Richardson was known as a man who helped traveling musicians by giving them money, food, and lodging. Throughout the twenties both Oklahoma City and Kansas City became central gathering places for jazz musicians. Ellison has noted, "much of the so-called Kansas City jazz was actually brought to perfection in Oklahoma by Oklahomans." (Anderson, 15)

In was in Oklahoma City that the Blue Devils played (made up of the early members of the soon-to-be-famous Count Basie band). Members included Oran "Hot Lips" Page, Edward Christian (brother of famed jazz guitarist Charlie Christian) and "Little Willie" Lewis, both on piano, Edward "Crack" McNeal on the drums, Lawrence "Inky" Williams, Ermuel "Gut Bucket" Coleman on trombone, and Jimmy Rushing—who would become Ellison's close friend—as vocalist.

The music had a strong impression on the life of Ralph Ellison; years later in a written tribute to Jimmy Rushing, he recalled those moments when the music filled the air of Deep Second:

> Everyone on Oklahoma City's East Side knew that sweet, high-floating sound.... For Jimmy Rushing was not simply a local entertainer, he expressed a value, an attitude about the world for which our lives afforded no other definition....

In those days I lived near the Rock Island roundhouse, where with a steady clanging of bells and a great groaning of wheels along the rails, switch engines made up the trains of freight unceasingly. Yet often in the late-spring night I could hear Rushing as I lay four blocks away in bed carrying to me as clear as a full-bored riff on "Hot Lips" Page's horn. Heard thus, across the dark blocks lined with locust trees, through the night throbbing with the natural aural imagery of the blues, with high-balling trains, departing bells, lonesome guitar chords simmering up from a shack in the alley—it was easy to imagine the voice as setting the pattern to which the instruments of the Blue Devils Orchestra and all the random sounds of the night arose, affirming, as it were, some ideal native to the time and to the land.... Jazz and the blues did not fit into the scheme of the things as spelled out by our two main institutions, the church and the school, but they gave expression to attitudes which found no place in these and helped to give our lives some semblance of wholeness. Jazz and the public dance was a third institution in our lives, and a vital one; and though Jimmy was far from being a preacher, he was, as official floor manager or master-of-the-dance at Slaughter's Hall, the leader of a public rite. (Anderson, 16-7)

Ellison not only listened to the music, but as his musical skills developed he played in gig bands under the leadership of Edward Christian. He was the only musician with a mellophone, and he often loaned the instrument to band members in exchange for sitting in on trumpet during rehearsal. (A mellophone is a brass instrument that resembles a large trumpet; french horn musicians play it in a marching band, and it has a similar range, and a similar tone.) Because he could read music and many band members could not, Ellison was often called upon to help interpret the music, but his involvement was limited by Ida Ellison who still kept a close rein on her son.

Ellison's job as a soda jerk at Randolph's Drug Store afforded still greater access to the musicians since the drugstore served as their daytime gathering place; they sat around and matched tales and stories, which gave him further insight into their everyday lives.

Despite the heavy influence of music in Ellison's life, literary arts too held a strong attraction. From his teacher Mrs. L. C. McFarland, he learned a great deal about the New Negro Movement of the twenties. Black writers like Langston Hughes, Countee Cullen, Claude McKay and James Weldon Jones inspired pride and also gave Ellison "a closer identification with poetry." (*Shadow*, 159)

Theater also played an important role in Deep Second. When the black actor Richard B. Harrison came to town and performed Shakespearean soliloquies on stage, the entire neighborhood turned out, and when white British actress Emma Bunting arrived in Oklahoma City, her black maid Miss Clark stayed in the Ellison home. It was from Miss Clark that Ellison learned about the inner workings of the theater and gained insight into British manners and customs.

Throughout his high school years, Ellison never lost his love for reading and was known to have his nose in a book at all times. In his senior year, he began reading the prefaces of George Bernard Shaw and became enamored with Shaw's writings.

While Ellison did not begin his writing career early, the seeds were planted. During his junior year at Douglass, he developed a bad cold that he couldn't shake. The school nurse ran into him on the street and upon hearing his bad cough insisted he go to the lung clinic at the hospital. Ellison found himself sitting in the waiting area among a large gathering of very ill people; he felt a sense of terror and fear and wanted to capture the moment on paper. The incident became his first vivid memory of being drawn to writing.

As graduation grew near, Ellison's desire to become a Renaissance man drew surprisingly close; one would be hard pressed to fully grasp the length, depth and breadth of his education. The teachers at Douglass High School had themselves been educated by dedicated teachers from New England who taught in the South during Reconstruction, and Ellison's transcript included four years of Latin taught by a black teacher who spoke fluent Latin, Greek, and Hebrew.

The unshakable foundation for Ralph Ellison, however, was his mother, Ida. Her role in his growth and development cannot be underestimated. She was an animated conversationalist, and continually engaged her boys in stimulating discussions. She worked to keep the memory of their father vivid by relating stories about his childhood, and she told of adventures from her childhood growing up on a

Georgia plantation. She was avidly concerned with political issues and candidly discussed them with Ellison and his younger brother.

Ida Ellison taught her sons to be tolerant of all people. During one occasion when Ellison was enraged at a woman who had started a rumor about him, his mother calmed him down by reminding him to consider the source of the rumor. "You've been working in drugstores and barbershops and at that office and since you've been around ..." she told him. "And ... as much as you have, you must know that she's crazy. So use your head. She doesn't have to be in an institution, but you have to understand and accept the fact that she isn't responsible." It was through this incident that he came to realize he could save "a lot of wear and tear with people if I just learned to understand them." (Graham, 274)

Upon graduation, Ellison won a state scholarship and decided to study music at Tuskegee Institute in Alabama; but first he would have to face the challenge of making the trip from Oklahoma to Alabama— a challenge Ellison met head on.

LEAVING THE TERRITORY

At the same time Ellison was preparing to set out on his own, the country was in the throes of the Great Depression and money was scarce. He received a letter from Tuskegee requesting him to arrive on a specific day in June because the school needed a trumpet player. The little he'd saved from his eight-dollar-a-week job as an elevator operator had gone to purchase a new trumpet and new clothes, leaving nothing for travel expenses, but he was determined to get to Alabama.

In desperation, Ellison turned to a friend of the Randolphs, a light-skinned black man named Charlie, who often passed for white when traveling. He was as small as a jockey, and he was adept at hoboing and constantly rode the rails in and out of Oklahoma City. Ellison asked Charlie's help to acquire this skill in order to get to Alabama, and Charlie agreed but only on the condition that Ellison secured his mother's permission. Ida was reluctant, but she finally did consent. She instructed Ellison to send word when he arrived safely, and then she would ship his clothes to him.

During the thirties, out-of-work men were forced to "ride the rails"—traveling about the country in search of work. They gathered in areas near the train stations that became known as "hobo jungles." Riding the rails was against the law and extremely dangerous; learning to do it safely was difficult, but Charlie taught Ellison how to board trains, who to avoid, and how to protect himself:

> You had to be able to read a manifest which was nailed on the side of the car to know where a train was going and when it was scheduled to be there. You had to know how to avoid railroad bulls (detectives). You had to know what to do when a train got into town and where there were difficult police or sheriffs. You had to know where you could buy things in a racial situation. (Graham, 249)

Riding the rails was difficult for a white man and even more dangerous for a black person. Charlie warned Ellison to avoid Arkansas because, should he get caught there, he could be imprisoned and put to work on a chain gang.

Wearing comfortable shoes, carrying an extra shirt, and a little extra money stuffed in his shoe, Ellison was ready to go. The trip went well for the first few days, but Charlie would accompany him only part of the way and they parted company in East Saint Louis.

By the time Ellison entered Alabama tensions were running high over the retrial of the Scottsboro boys. Two years earlier nine black boys had been taken from a train bound for Chattanooga Tennessee. The young men ranged in age from 12 to 20 and did not know each other; they were accused of raping and beating two white girls. The boys were taken to the Jackson County Jail in Scottsboro, Alabama, hence the name Scottsboro boys. Crowds gathered outside the jail and threatened to lynch all nine of the boys. A speedy, unfair trial resulted in a death sentence for all with the exception of the twelve-year-old. The International Labor Defense, an arm of the Communist Party in America, then came to the boys' defense.

The outside interference angered locals and tensions surrounding the trial were heightened by a wave of lynchings, violence, and cross-burnings throughout the South. (It would later be proved that both girls—one a prostitute—had lied about all the allegations.)

It was at the time of the second Scottsboro trial that Ellison entered the state and, because of the excessive publicity involved in the case, he was well aware of the situation. At Decatur, Alabama, Ellison was discovered by railroad detectives and ordered to line up on the tracks along with 40 or 50 hoboes—he was terrified, and when several of the men broke and ran, he threw his lot in with them and ran too, "far closer to the ground than I had ever managed to do as a high school football running back." While he was able to escape unharmed, he remembered the incident for the rest of his life "the fear, the horror and sense of helplessness before legal injustice." (Busby, 6) It took Ellison approximately a week to travel from Oklahoma to Tuskegee, Alabama where he would soon learn that he'd entered a whole new world, both on campus and off.

Booker T. Washington founded the Tuskegee Institute in 1891, and it was originally designed as a trade school for young African Americans to learn marketable skills. Washington believed it important that blacks be prepared to take the jobs that were available to them. "It is at the bottom of life we must begin," he stated, "not at the top." (Busby, 7)

Washington stood strongly against the mass migration of blacks from the South; he encouraged them to "Cast down your buckets where you are. Cast down in agriculture, mechanics, in commerce, in domestic service, and in the professions." (O'Meally, 14) His willingness to keep African Americans in a position of subservience to paternalistic whites brought him favor with Tuskegee's white patrons. By the time Ralph Ellison arrived on campus in 1933, much had changed with regard to the curriculum, but black acceptance of limitations in life remained strongly entrenched in the ideology of faculty and student body.

Composer William L. Dawson, head of the music department, saw to it that only the best black teachers served on the faculty in his department. Music majors had the choice of studying to become teachers or concert artists. Like Douglass High School, Tuskegee's music department boasted a choir, two glee clubs, an orchestra, and a concert band. Ellison traveled with the orchestra, and during a trip to Chicago he experienced his first opera.

Ellison had ten years of musical experience, which served him well under the rigors of Dawson's music department. As a freshman, he was required to practice three hours daily on his major instrument and one hour a day on his minor instrument. Additionally, classes were required in solfeggio (ear-training and sight-singing), harmony, and conducting. Juniors and seniors were required to play in the school orchestra and other ensemble groups.

Among the more gifted faculty members at Tuskegee was Professor of music, Hazel Harrison. "Harrison was a concert pianist who had been one of Ferrucio Busoni's prize pupils in Berlin and who had known Egon Petri Sergei, Prokofiev, Percy Grainger, and other leading musicians of her time." (O'Meally, 20) Ellison would later attribute Miss Harrison with teaching him a great deal about music and music appreciation.

Jazz was not taught in Tuskegee's music department, but it continued to be a vital part of Ellison's life. He played off-campus in a number of bands, and secured gigs in clubs in Columbus, Georgia, among other places.

Attitude and vision at Tuskegee may have been limited, but the campus library was not so, and for the better part of a year Ellison worked in the library and browsed the stacks where he discovered many books not introduced to him in the classroom. In these surroundings he set about on a course of self-study, beginning with T.S. Eliot's *The Waste Land*, which as he said, "seized his mind." Later he would look back on that discovery as a turning point in his life. Of *The Waste Land*, he wrote:

> Somehow its rhythms were often closer to those of jazz than were those of the Negro poets, and even though I could not understand then, its range of allusion was as mixed and as varied as that of Louis Armstrong. Yet there were its discontinuities, its changes of pace and its hidden system of organization, which escaped me. (*Shadow*, 160)

A fascination with *The Waste Land* led him to look up the references he found in the footnotes to the poem, which in turn led him to study writing technique for poetry and novel writing. He found the discipline was similar to the study of music only it was more enjoyable since it "involved no deadlines or credits." (*Shadow*, 160) "That really was a beginning of my literary education and, actually, it was the beginning of my transformation (or shall we say, meta-morphosis) from a would-be composer into some sort of novelist." (Busby, 8,9)

Reading led him to modernists such as Ezra Pound, Gertrude Stein, Ford Madox Ford, James Joyce, F. Scott Fitzgerald, and Ernest Hemingway, and from there he was drawn to nineteenth-century

writers such as Mark Twain and Herman Melville. He tried his hand at
poetry writing, and would later admit that he never wrote a decent
poem. "... But the conscious concern with writing began there at
Tuskegee: again without my being conscious that it was a forecast of
what I was going to do. It was a kind of innocent wordplay." (Graham,
90)

Living in Alabama, Ellison had his first real taste of a more
rigorously enforced segregation than he had previously experienced; for
instance, the movie theater had separate entrances with a white side and
a black side. Ellison referred to it as a "product of social absurdity."
(O'Meally, 11) and also stated that it made no difference to him since
he went to view the movie and not to see the white folk.

Racial attitudes in the South forced Ellison to play roles that were
distasteful to him, but he fought back by retaining his own inward
presence; he learned to "outmaneuver those who interpreted my silence
as submissions, my efforts at self-control as fear, my contempt as awe
before superior status, my dreams of faraway places and room at the top
of the heap as defeat before the barriers of their stifling, provincial
world." (O'Meally, 10)

Almost as disturbing as the segregation Ellison had experienced
were the restrictions found in the black community in the South. Young
African Americans were taught from childhood that the actions of one
affected all and as a result individuality was stifled. By his third year at
Tuskegee, Ellison was dabbling in arts other than music and poetry. He
enrolled in classes for watercolor and found he had a natural inclination
for working in the three-dimensional medium of sculpture. Within a
few weeks, he'd created several clay portraits of close friends.

A mix-up in his scholarship funding found Ellison completing his
junior year with the prospect of no tuition money for the coming fall
term. Rather than try to work and save money in Alabama, he made the
bold decision to go to New York, and not just to New York, but to
Harlem, the place that had become real to him in the stories he'd heard,
the literature he'd read, and the people he'd studied. The Harlem he'd
heard about was "a glamorous place, a place where wonderful music
existed and where there was a great tradition of Negro American style
and elegance." (O'Meally, 26) In fact, Harlem was the place that would
become his home for most of the remainder of his life.

HARLEM

While Ralph Ellison was still a barefoot boy growing up in Oklahoma City in the 1920s, Harlem was experiencing an unprecedented outburst of creative artistic activity among its African-American population. Known as the Harlem Renaissance, the movement exalted the unique culture of the blacks, celebrated their heritage, and spoke of "The New Negro," a term coined by Alain LeRoy Locke, Professor of philosophy at Howard and one of the theorists of the Harlem Renaissance; his book entitled *The New Negro* was published in 1925.

Locke maintained the New Negro was one who "has been transformed from a dependent ward into a self-reliant, self-respecting citizen of the democracy." (*Black American Writers*, 162) He saw the New Negro as one with an awakened racial pride, and predicted there would be a blossoming of arts. His prediction was to come true during the Harlem Renaissance.

Black urban migration combined with a societal trend toward artistic experimentation, and the rise of black intellectuals such as Locke, Marcus Garvey and W.E.B. DuBois worked to spur the success of black artists. Additionally it became socially fashionable for wealthy white patrons to sponsor and offer financial aid to young black artists. The movement began with literature, but soon carried over into music, painting, sculpture, dramatic revues and plays.

Ellison learned about these black artists both in high school and college, and their names were as familiar to him as those of close friends. When he arrived in Harlem on July 6, 1936, he carried with him a letter of introduction from his art teacher Eva Hamlin to Augusta Savage, a black sculptor who lived in Harlem, and it gave a measure of comfort to know he had at least one connection in the city.

His first stop was the Harlem Annex of the YMCA where he rented a room. The next morning upon rising, he went across the street to eat breakfast, and to his joy and amazement, he found Langston Hughes and Alain Locke. Hughes was recognizable from pictures he'd seen, and Locke he recognized because the man had recently been at Tuskegee to visit Hazel Harrison.

Not one to miss such an opportunity, Ellison approached the two men and asked Locke if he remembered him from their brief introduction at the college. Locke did remember him and introduced him to Langston Hughes. In the course of the conversation, Ellison asked Hughes if he knew of a black writer by the name of Richard Wright, two of whose poems "I Have Seen Black Hands" and "Between the World and Me" had inspired and made him curious to meet the author.

Hughes did know Wright, and informed him that the poet would soon be moving to New York to edit a new magazine, *New Challenge*. Wright was subsequently briefed by Hughes about Ellison's interest and he sent a card saying, "Dear Ralph Ellison, Langston Hughes tells me that you're interested in meeting me," he also told him how he could be reached. (Busby, 10)

Before the men parted company on that fateful morning in Harlem, Hughes asked Ellison to return a few library books he was carrying with him, and suggested he read the books before returning them. The two books were *Days of Wrath* and *Man's Fate* by André Malraux; they made a strong impression on Ellison and would later play an important role in his writing and his life.

When Wright arrived in the city, Ellison met him and the two became friends and literary sounding boards for one another.

He made contact with Savage, but the sculptor was so busy with the Work's Progress Administration (WPA) she had no time to take on extra students, so Ellison turned to Harlem artist Richmond Barthé and studied under his direction for a year and a half before deciding his talents did not lie there.

Ellison's skill as a musician did not prove to be profitable although he had originally hoped to find a position playing with a Harlem band and very nearly made it—one day he was invited by a friend to Duke Ellington's apartment. As with Alain Locke, Duke Ellington had made a recent visit to Tuskegee where the two had been introduced. As they talked, Ellington invited him to attend a rehearsal the next day, but later cancelled the invitation. Ellison didn't want to be presumptuous and never pursued the matter, so the opportunity was lost.

Lack of funds prevented Ellison from joining the musician's union, which put yet another roadblock in the path to finding work, and that, coupled with the fact that hundreds of skilled musicians were out of work, discouraged him even further. Steady employment was almost impossible to find during the Depression years and he made do with a succession of odd jobs wherever he could find them. For a time he worked in the food bar at the YMCA using skills he'd learned in high school as a waiter and barman, and between jobs he often slept on a park bench in Central Park.

One job that proved more interesting than the rest was that of substitute file clerk in the office of psychiatrist, Harry Stack Sullivan. As Ellison glanced through the case histories, it sparked in him a new interest in modern psychology and he began to revisit Freud, paying special attention to the subject of dreams and their effects.

Early in 1937, Ellison received the devastating news that his mother, who was living in Dayton, Ohio, was seriously ill. He was almost penniless but he traveled to Dayton where he and his brother attended to their mother until she died. After her funeral Ellison stayed on in Dayton for almost seven months.

During the cold winter months, Ellison and his brother hunted quail together in the snow-covered fields outside Dayton. Some of the birds they cooked and ate; others they sold to officials at the General Motors plant. The quail represented their livelihood and hitting the birds with a wing shot was vitally important. "I had been hunting since I was eleven," Ellison said, "but no one had broken down the process of wing-shooting for me and it was from reading Hemingway that I learned to lead a bird." (Busby, 12) Thus it was Hemingway's description of leading a bird in flight that made him an excellent shot.

In the evenings, Ellison read extensively and began to diligently practice his writing skills. Hemingway's works had a profound effect on him and many of his early attempts were patterned after Hemingway's style. It would take years for Ellison to find his own literary form and voice.

The loss of Ida Ellison was extremely difficult, mainly because her death was so senseless; Ida had fallen from a porch and an inept black doctor, without ever taking an x-ray, diagnosed her as having arthritis. She suffered from intense pain and soon died from tuberculosis of the hip. Ellison cited the incident often throughout his life and used it as an example of how important it is to learn one's craft, no matter what that craft might be.

Not only did Ellison love his mother, he admired her and held her in the highest regard; his references to her in later years were highly complimentary. While he was away at college, he learned that Ida had been purposely violating a segregated-housing ordinance in Oklahoma

City; she would rent a place, the police would arrest and throw her in jail and, after the NAACP bailed her out, she would go back and do it all over again. "She had that kind of forthrightness," he said, "and I like to think that that was much more valuable than anything literary that she gave me." (Graham, 276)

He saw his mother as having helped him escape the "limitations of trying to impose any ingroup class distinctions upon the people of my community.... Her background and attitudes were such that all kinds of people came into the house, and or we visited their houses. That was one of the enriching parts of my experience ...". (Graham, 275) He would later note that even Ida's tolerance of his interest in jazz and his desire to spend time with the jazz musicians, had worked to shape his life—because it was jazz rather than the classical music that developed his artistic dedication and enabled him to become a published author. He owed so much of who he was to his mother, and though he'd been away from her for several years, her death left a deep void in his life.

Upon his return to Harlem, Ellison's friendship with Wright grew as he spent a good deal of time at the office of the *Daily Worker*. At this time the only writing he had done was college assignments and he was in awe of Wright who was already published. To his credit, Wright accepted Ellison on equal footing and the two spent hours discussing the many facets of literature and art. It was at Wright's urging that Ellison wrote his first book review for *New Challenge* magazine. For the assignment, he chose *The Low Grounds* by Waters Edward Turpin. The review appeared in the fall 1937 issue and became his first published piece.

When the subsequent issue was found lacking a short fiction piece, Wright challenged Ellison to write one. "You talk well about stories. Why don't you try?" (Busby, 12) The invitation seemed made to order, since Ellison had been experimenting with short-story plots for the past few months. He had been entertaining the thought of leaving music behind and channeling all his energies into writing.

His short story, based on his experience riding the rails from Oklahoma to Alabama, was entitled "Hymie's Bull." The story was accepted by Wright and set into galley proofs; however, the magazine folded before the story could be printed. Ellison still had a copy of the proofs in his possession at the time of his death in 1994. Regardless of whether or not the story was published, the die had been cast. From that point Ellison went on to write a series of published book reviews, as well as political and social essays, and by 1939 his first short story was published, entitled, "Slick Gonna Learn."

Although Ellison turned from music to writing he did not abandon music altogether. He was drawn by the innovative jazz music being played at places like the Apollo, the Savoy Ballroom, the Renaissance Ballroom, Smalls Paradise, and Minton's Playhouse—where bebop allegedly was born—and spent many evenings (sometimes all night long) dancing or listening in on jam sessions. He was a friend of artists like Dizzy Gillespie, Sarah Vaughn, Fats Navarro, Clark Terry, and Teddy Wilson.

After Ellison married he lived next door to Teddy Wilson, a musician who played at Café Society Downtown. The two men and their wives often hung out at after-hours clubs, where the jamming went on until dawn. Ellison could never be far from music; it would always be an integral part of his life. In later years, he would write extensively on the subject.

Through his friendship with Wright, Ellison was able to get a job with the WPA. While the Depression was an extremely difficult time for African Americans, ironically, it was also a time of advancement due to the many government programs. Ellison would later describe it as a "gift of freedom arrived in the guise of a disaster." (Busby, 13) The job meant that he would enjoy a steady paycheck, and the $103.50 a month he was paid added up to much more than what the odd jobs had been paying. But in the end, Ellison gained much more than a steady paycheck; his years with the WPA spanned from 1938 to 1942, and provided Ellison an opportunity to write, to study writing, to interact with other professional writers, and best of all he was paid for it. In addition, it left evenings free to study and work on his own writing. It was the ideal opportunity at the ideal time.

Ellison joined with about twenty other writers in a project called *The Negro in New York* that dealt with prominent black New Yorkers and incidents involving the black community. Research took him to the shelves of the Schaumburg Library where he produced footnoted pieces such as, "Negro Instructors in New York Institutions of Higher Learning," and "Great Riots of New York; Complete Account of the Four Days of Draft Riot of 1863."

By far his favorite project was the "Living Lore Unit" which took him into the streets and back alleys of Harlem, collecting "the tales, toasts, boasts, songs, and rhymes of American folklore." (O'Meally, 34) Questioning small children, he sought to discover where they learned their rhymes and tales. He visited hundreds of Harlem apartments and public places, interviewing adults and paying particular attention to their speech patterns and idiosyncrasies.

He managed to have the stories recorded, "by using a kind of Hemingway typography, by using the repetitions." Then he added, "I couldn't quite get the tone of the sounds in but I could get some of the patterns and get an idea of what it was like." (O'Meally, 34)

The importance of folklore in everyday life, and therefore in literature, began to emerge in Ellison's thinking and the next step was to learn to weave it adeptly into his own writing. At the same time, he was reading Henry James, Joseph Conrad, and rereading Mark Twain. "Any writer," he said, "who wrote about the craft." (Graham, 295) In retrospect he could see that it all fit perfectly together.

Ellison's approach was to work with his writing just as he worked with his music, and involved training, study, and hours of practice. Much of his early writing was shown to no one. "Some of the first things were embarrassing," he admitted. "You go from something that you've read, until you find out about how *you* feel about it." (Graham, 294)

The disappointment for Ellison was finding that well-known African-American writers of the time had no background in literature. "I could not discuss technique with them," he said, "and even though we shared some points of ideology, because a number of them were leftists, they couldn't talk to me about technical matters." (Graham, 294)

In June of 1938, while interviewing a black man on 135th Street and Lenox Avenue, Ellison heard a folktale about "Sweet-the-Monkey," who could make himself invisible, break into the homes of white folks, and take their things—not because he needed them but just to show he could do it. The theme of invisibility, as well as much of the folklore he collected, would have a direct effect on Ellison's future writing career.

During his first few years in New York, Ellison was affected not only by the literary arts but also by politics. His friend Richard Wright was a member of the Communist Party, as were other influential blacks. In 1937, Langston Hughes traveled to Russia and later wrote about what he saw of interracial cooperation there.

In spite of the fact that Ellison demonstrated, picketed, and wrote a number of articles supporting the Party, he never came to a point where he completely trusted the Communists. While they purported to support the arts, he observed them elevating politics above the arts in almost every situation.

The unique problems of the Depression prompted a new pattern of class-consciousness that arose among the working-class black population. Thus, the black writers attempted to be the voice for the masses crying out for justice. Ellison did not succumb to such protest writing and wanted to teach others to do the same. "In years to come, he would continue to advise writers to sharpen their writing technique, to acquaint themselves with history and psychology, and to resist the temptation of presenting mere black stereotypes. Only the well-informed and skillful writer could present a sharply focused—a truly realistic—picture of black experience." (O'Meally, 41)

His views did not make him good material for the Communist Party, nor did they win him many friends in the black literary community. From early on Ellison seemed to fit no one mold. "I never accepted the ideology which *The New Masses* tried to impose on writers. They hated Dostoyevsky, but I was studying Dostoyevsky. They felt that Henry James was a decadent, some sort of snob who had nothing to teach a writer from the lower classes—I was studying James." (Graham, 124)

THE WAR YEARS

Much of Ralph Ellison's earliest published work is made up of book reviews written for magazines like *New Challenge, Direction, Negro Quarterly,* and *New Masses.* In the spring of 1940, he jumped at the opportunity to travel to Washington, D.C. with five other writers and attend the Third National Negro Congress. Ellison wrote an article printed in *New Masses* about his experience entitled "A Congress Jim Crow Didn't Attend."

In the article he voiced protests against the issues facing blacks—exploitation of workers, segregated housing, segregated public facilities, and lynchings. For the most part, he could see the advantage of grassroots movements. "... In the faces of my people I saw strength," he wrote. "There with the whites in the audience I saw the positive

forces of civilization and the best guarantee of America's future."
(O'Meally, 54)

During the years spent working for the WPA, Ellison also spent a
good deal of time at the offices of *Negro Quarterly*, a magazine founded
by Angelo Herndon. In 1942, Herndon invited Ellison to come on
board at the magazine as the managing editor, promising him the same
salary made at the WPA. Ellison accepted, but the promise fell through;
the pay was irregular and after a year the magazine folded.

In August 1943, a riot broke out in Harlem following an
altercation in a bar between a policeman, and a black soldier, the
soldier's mother and wife. The situation deteriorated rapidly, and for a
day and a night the looting and burning went on with many businesses
and shops—both black and white—being destroyed. Ellison covered the
riot for the *New York Post* and later would use the incident as the basis
for a scene in his book, *Invisible Man*.

By this time, America had entered World War II after the
bombing of Pearl Harbor in 1941. Many blacks across the country were
disgruntled when President Roosevelt implemented a segregated Army.
The Communist Party's war policies supported the segregated armed
forces, and Ellison made his last break with the organization. Early in
the war Ellison attempted to join the Navy band, a place where he could
revisit his love of music. However, by the time he attempted to sign up,
no more musicians were needed. He wanted to contribute to the war
effort, but because he wanted nothing to do with a "Jim Crow army,"
Ellison joined the Merchant Marines as a "second cook. I was in charge
of making breakfast, and I also turned out cornbread, biscuits and fried
pies." (Graham, 380)

In wartime, merchant ships were relied upon to carry supplies to
fighting forces scattered around the globe; they were crucial to the war
effort. Although not equipped for battle, the ships were constantly
under attack and faced danger from submarines, mines, armed raiders
and destroyers, aircraft, kamikaze pilots, and the elements. Nearly
7,300 mariners were killed at sea during the course of the war, 12,000
were wounded, and at least 1,100 died from their wounds.

Between stints at sea, Ellison spent leave at home in New York.
During one such leave, he met a girl named Fanny McConnell. It was
at the suggestion of a friend that the two become acquainted. "He and
I had a mutual friend," Fanny remembered, "who kept telling me about

Ralph's wonderful library." "I adored books. And writing *had* been my first love." (Anderson, 27)

The two talked on the phone and decided to meet at Frank's Restaurant on 125th Street. He told her the color of his coat, and she told him the color of her dress. For dinner, she chose the cheapest item on the menu—chicken à la king, and as he did not want to embarrass her, Ellison ordered the same thing. The two quickly connected with each other and food was soon forgotten. Through the course of the evening they found they held much in common and began writing to one another while Ellison was at sea.

There had been a previous marriage for Ellison when he was younger, but it ended quickly when his in-laws insisted that he forego his dreams and take a job in the post office. He found he could not exist within the confines of such small thinking.

Fanny, he found, not only shared his dreams but also became a source of encouragement to him. She had been born in Louisville, Kentucky, and grew up in Pueblo, Colorado and Chicago. She attended Fisk University in Nashville, Tennessee, where she worked as a secretary for James Weldon Johnson, a poet and diplomat, who was one of the founders of the NAACP.

Not a shy girl, Fanny had written to Johnson telling him of her desire to write and asked his help in obtaining a job. Not only did he hire her as a secretary, he later helped her obtain a fellowship to the University of Iowa where she studied drama and speech. After graduation, she returned to Chicago where she founded a small theater group. Subsequently, a job with the Urban League brought her to New York and soon after that she met Ralph Ellison. For a time she had entertained thoughts of becoming a writer herself, but after meeting Ellison she felt she lacked the dedication. "I did not have the sustaining power or the memory," she confessed. (Anderson, 27)

Ellison continued to work diligently on his writing even while at sea, tackling the daunting task of a full-length novel. In 1944, he applied for a fellowship from the Julius Rosenwald Fund and was accepted; the money received meant he was financially solvent for the first time in many years.

His novel was based on stories he'd heard from his friends from Tuskegee who served in the U.S. Army Air Corps. The main character, a black American pilot, is shot down over Germany and taken as a prisoner-of-war. He is the highest-ranking officer, which causes racial tension among the white prisoners, and creates a situation that the German commander uses for his own amusement. Ellison used the theme to demonstrate the dilemmas faced by blacks thrown into certain situations. The novel was never published, partly because he was never satisfied with the way it turned out.

Several of Ellison's short stories were published while he was in the military. Two of the more popular ones were "King of the Bingo Game" (1944) and "Flying Home" (1944). Thus he began making a name for himself as a short story writer.

A classmate of Ellison's from Tuskegee, Albert Murray, was stationed at the Tuskegee Army Air Field during the war and the two men established a renewed friendship and began corresponding with one another. Their friendship grew through the years and extended to the time of Ellison's death.

Murray happened to read "Flying Home" in *Cross Section* and was amused by an incident in the story where an airman had to crash-land a plane after flying into a buzzard. Murray sat down to write Ralph that one of their planes had actually flown into an Alabama buzzard—after the story had been published. Since it was a twin-engine bomber, there was no crash-landing, but the coincidence was amazing.

While Ellison was delighted at the coincidence he was not really surprised. Writing back to Murray, he said that, "stories endure not only from generation to generation but also from age to age because literary truth amounts to prophecy. Telling is not only a matter of retelling but also of foretelling." (*Trading Twelves*, xxiii)

Ellison's next voyage during the winter of 1944 took him across the North Atlantic, delivering supplies for troops during the Battle of the Bulge. On that trip, he contracted a kidney infection from contaminated water on the ship and the condition continued to plague him throughout the return voyage. In the summer of 1945, upon doctor's orders, he took sick leave and traveled to a friend's farm in Waitsfield, Vermont to rest. At the time, he was reading *The Hero* by Lord Ragland and "speculating on the nature of Negro leadership in the U.S. ...." (Graham, 14)

In the warm weather, he set up his typewriter in the open doorway of an old barn overlooking the green hills of Vermont. He was struggling with his prison camp novel, which wasn't coming together as well as he'd hoped. His reading of *The Hero*, spawned "images of incest and murder, dissolution and rebirth whirled in my head," he said, images that kept distracting him. (Busby, 15) Rolling a fresh sheet of paper into his typewriter, he typed these words, "I am an invisible man." At first he started to destroy the paper, but then began to wonder what type of person might write those words and why:

> And suddenly I could hear in my head a blackface comedian bragging on the stage of Harlem's Apollo Theatre to the effect that each generation of his family was becoming so progressively black of complexion that no one, not even its own mother, had ever been able to see the two-year-old baby. The audience had roared with laughter and I recognized something of the same joking, in-group, Negro American irony sounding from my rumpled page. Slowly, like an image surfacing from the layers of an exposed Polaroid exposure, a shadow of the speaker arose in my mind and I grasped at his range of implication. (Busby, 16)

Thus he began the novel that would launch his writing career.

PRODUCING A CLASSIC

Ralph Ellison and Fanny McConnell were married in 1946 and settled down in Harlem. "We combined libraries," Ralph would say in an interview years later. (Graham, 296) It amazed the both of them to learn that they had saved the same identical back copy of *Vanity Fair*. Ellison had been reading the magazine since childhood when his mother would bring home discarded copies from the homes where she cleaned for white families.

Fanny Ellison was supportive of her husband's artistic efforts, and she was willing to work to help earn money while Ellison labored over his novel. She served as the executive director of the American Medical Center for Burma, an organization that promoted the work of Dr. Gordon S. Seagrave, known as the "Burma Surgeon."

Ellison's fascination with radios as a child spurred him to learn how to build high-fidelity amplifiers and install sound systems, and by doing this along with selling his color photography and published book

reviews, he supplemented the household budget. An extended
Rosenwald grant and monthly support from art patron, Mrs. J. Caesar
Guggenheimer, also aided his efforts.

Work on the novel stretched into years. By 1949, Ralph and Fanny
Ellison were living in a small ground-floor apartment sandwiched
between a restaurant with a noisy jukebox, and a "night-employed
swing enthusiast" who in the daytime hours played Count Basie songs
so loud it nearly blasted his typewriter off the table. From the back alley
he could hear the singing drunks who'd just come out of the corner bar,
and upstairs lived a singer. "... You might say we had a singer on the
ceiling," he quipped. (*Shadow*, 189)

It was then that he decided to install his own stereophonic system
and wired music throughout the apartment. "There were wires and
pieces of equipment all over the tiny apartment (I became a compulsive
experimenter) and it was worth your life to move about without first
taking careful bearings." (*Shadow*, 195) The distractions were thus
eliminated and the novel progressed.

Invisible Man found a home with editors Frank Taylor and Albert
Erskine at Reynal & Hitchcock; and when they moved to Random
House in 1947, the contract for the book went with them. Later, Taylor
left to find his fortune in Hollywood and Erskine remained in the
position of Ellison's editor.

Erskine showed chapters of *Invisible Man* to Cyril Connolly, editor
of the English magazine *Horizon*, who published an excerpt in the
October 1947 issue. The next year the same section appeared in
Magazine of the Year. Initial reactions to the work were favorable.

By 1950, Ellison was borrowing an office from friends Beatrice
and Francis Steegmuller. He kept regular office hours, arriving at 608
Fifth Avenue early each morning, taking the elevator to the eighth
floor, and working until late each evening. In a letter to Al Murray,
March 1950, he mentioned that the book was almost finished, however,
it would be another year before the final draft was actually delivered in
April 1951—the book was seven years in the making. "... Strange to
say," he wrote Al, "I've been depressed ever since—starting with a high
fever that developed during the evening we were clearing up the final
typing. I suppose crazy things will continue to happen until that
crowning craziness, publication." (*Trading Twelves*, 16)

Through the summer, galley proofs were read aloud with friends.
Ellison's own edits cut 200 pages, reducing it to 606 pages. Advance

copies were due to go to reviewers before the actual spring 1952 publication date.

The book finally appeared on the market and it took the country by storm, surprising some, angering others, and managing to stay on the best-seller list for 13 weeks. For a work coming from a relatively unknown author, the coverage was quite extensive. Most reviewers realized that it was a significant publication, noting that it went far beyond what any black author had done before him.

Webster Schott of the Kansas City *Star* wrote, "It's a paradox, but the quality which classifies Ralph Ellison's *Invisible Man* as one of the best novels yet written by an American Negro is that it's concerned with themes which are ... universal rather than racial." (*Black American Writers* Vol II, 54) Still another stated, "it is about being colored in a white society and yet manages not to be a grievance book." (*Black American Writers* Vol II, 55) Saul Bellow called it a "book of the very first order, a superb book ... tragicomic, poetic, the tone of the very strongest sort of creative intelligence." (Busby, 16) Nearly every favorable review (which remained in the majority) pointed out the universality of the novel, that it dealt with all mankind and not just with African Americans.

Reviews from the black community were also primarily favorable. Leftist publications, however, were anything but kind. John O. Killens stated in *Freedom* "Negro people need Ralph Ellison's *Invisible Man* like we need a hole in the head or a stab in the back" and called it "a vicious distortion of Negro life." (Busby, 17)

To those blacks who felt Ellison had hedged on his role as a voice for his people, he said, "If the Negro, or any other writer, is going to do what is expected of him, he's lost the battle before he takes the field ... Too many books by Negro writers are addressed to a white audience. By doing this the authors run the risk of limiting themselves to the audience's presumptions of what a Negro should be ...." (Ellison, *Shadow*, 170)

All along, it had been Ellison's goal to portray the richness and fullness of black life in America and the importance of black folk tradition in defining the black person. He was determined to illustrate the blending of black and white cultures in America, and realized that he personified the theory and was himself a product of all the great writers of the past.

In a 1971 interview, Ralph—who had by then been using the term Negro American for many years—insisted that he used it as a description of "mixed racial heritage" and "pluralistic cultural background." Reminding readers that the novel is a universal form, he explained that he wrote out of a total conscious awareness of American literature as well as "Russian, French, English and German literature." He went on to say that he "couldn't have written certain sentences but for the fact that certain white writers wrote certain sentences." Then he stated that the reverse was true: "William Faulkner couldn't have written certain dialogues but for having heard certain *black* Mississippians expressing themselves in certain succinct ways." (Graham, 207)

Regardless of the reviews—favorable or unfavorable—readers kept buying the book, and as Ellison's fame began to spread invitations for speaking engagements poured in. One such trip to North Carolina involved newspaper interviews, photos, television shows and a speech at vespers for Bennett's Homemaking Institute where the church atmosphere gave him an acute case of homesickness and nostalgia. He and the preacher entered the sanctuary from behind the choir loft where the organ bellows are operated, and in a flash he remembered playing in just such a passageway as a little child. "I know all of the hymns," he wrote to Al Murray, "and the whole order of service and in spite of everything the emotions started striking past my defenses, not a religious emotion, but that of *remembering* religious feeling ...." (*Trading Twelves*, 42)

To add to the nostalgia, he had a reunion with family members— cousins and aunts and uncles—some of whom he'd never met, and while there he was able to identify obvious family traits. One relative related a story about his grandfather, who had once stood up against a mob of whites and prevented a friend from being lynched; this was the same grandfather he remembered visiting when he was only four.

A year after the appearance of *Invisible Man*, in July 1953, Ellison was invited to return to Oklahoma City, making contact with many of the friends with whom he'd grown up. The city had expanded and changed a great deal, and one of the biggest changes were new neighborhoods where blacks were now able to live. "...There are several new additions financed by Negroes," he observed, "and for the first time in the history of the city large numbers of Negroes are living in houses which were never the whites' to abandon." (*Trading Twelves*, 51)

He spent time with the Randolph-Slaughter family looking through old picture albums and reliving the memories of times past. Deep Second as he had known it was gone forever and for that he grieved, but it was still a jazz town, and the sound of the freight trains sounded as good to him as they did "when I lay on a pallet in the moon-drenched kitchen door and listened and dreamed of the time when I would leave and see the world." (*Trading Twelves*, 51)

No matter how good the memories in Oklahoma City, Harlem was now his home and he was more than ready to return. Harlem, he had once remarked, gave him room to discover who he was. Additionally, he felt he had to live close to other black people. "Why do I live always close to other Negroes? Because I have to hear the language," he explained. "My medium is language, and there is a Negro idiom, in fact there are many Negro idioms in the American language. I have to hear that sounding in my ears. I have to." (Graham, 91)

Within a year of publication, *Invisible Man* received the Russwurm Award, the Certificate of Award from the *Chicago Defender*, and the coveted National Book Award; the latter was an unheard of accomplishment for a first novel and the citation from the jury made up of Martha Foley, Irving Howe, Howard Mumford Jones, and Alfred Kazin read in part:

> In it (the book) he shows us how invisible we all are to each other. With a positive exuberance of narrative gifts, he has broken away from the conventions and patterns of the tight "well-made" novel. Mr. Ellison has the courage to take many literary risks, and he has succeeded with them. (Graham, 99)

Ellison *had* taken literary risks with his novel, and in his acceptance speech on January 28, 1953, he explained that he'd found existing forms of the novel either too restrictive or too filled with social cynicism and understatement. He needed a novel with a broader and deeper range, and his search led him to the famous nineteenth-century novelists; writers such as Mark Twain, who "took a much greater responsibility for the condition of democracy and, indeed, their works were imaginative projections of the conflicts within the human heart which arose when the sacred principles of the Constitution and the Bill of Rights clashed with the practical exigencies of human greed and fear, hate and love." (Ellison, *Shadow*, 104)

While the term "classic" became quickly attached to *Invisible Man*, Ellison remained passively surprised at the label. "It was just a book I wrote," he said. "I didn't have anything to lose. I didn't think that I was writing a classic. I didn't think the book would sell." (*Black American Writers* Vol II, 47) But sell it did and for the next thirty years the book was never out of print.

Even though he felt emotionally spent after the publication of his novel, Ellison began jotting notes for a second novel almost before the first one was off the press. When asked about his next book, he commented it might be on the same theme, stating that he didn't feel he had exhausted the theme of invisibility; he even believed there were edited pieces of the first book that could be salvaged for the second.

YEARS OF CONFLICT

With a best seller to his credit, Ellison began to receive invitations to speak and teach at a number of universities. At first he felt obligated to accept, and by the spring of 1954, he had lined up speaking engagements at Tuskegee, Dillard, Bethune-Cookman and Howard University—all in one trip. However, he found the pay was bad and the pace too hectic, and soon learned to be more selective.

In the fall of that same year, he won a Rockefeller Foundation Award and held a lecture tour in Germany, afterward traveling to Austria where he spoke at the Salzburg Seminar on American Studies. For the next few years, his main source of income came from teaching and from speaking engagements.

In 1955, Ellison received word that he had been awarded Prix de Rome Fellowships from the American Academy of Arts and Letters, which meant he and Fanny would live in Rome for two years. Coincidentally, during the same time, his friend Al Murray along with his wife Mozelle and twelve-year-old daughter Michele (nicknamed Mique) were stationed by the Air Force in Casablanca. The Murrays arrived at the air base in August 1955, and the Ellisons arrived in Rome in October 1955.

By January, Fanny Ellison had suffered from an appendicitis attack and Ellison himself had spent eight days in bed from bronchial pneumonia. He attributed his illness to the dampness in the air and the filth in the streets and while he enjoyed the warm-hearted, friendly Italian people, he was somewhat disappointed in Europe as a whole. The longer he stayed abroad, the better America looked.

At one point he was attempting to cook "a mess of pigs' feet," and scoured Rome to find the pickling spices necessary, but without luck. "The next time somebody says something about Roman culture they're going to have to get a cop to stop me from talking," he wrote to Al Murray, "imagine a city without pickling spice." (*Trading Twelves*, 154)

Fanny Ellison found a job using her limited Berlitz Italian; the Catholic Church had founded an organization called La Lampada della Fraternita, which was a veteran's organization, and a clerk was needed to set up the office files. Fanny stepped in and accomplished the task with her usual finesse.

During the summer of 1956, the Ellisons and the Murrays met in Rome and traveled together on a trip that included Florence, Venice, Switzerland, Paris, and Madrid. On the last leg of the tour, the Ellisons departed for England and stayed in London for a week at the invitation of the P.E.N. Congress. The week was a whirlwind of social events including a reception with the Lord Mayor, lunch with the American Ambassador, lunch with the Mayor of Brighton, tea with the President of the House of Lords, and rubbing elbows with the literary elite of that time. Ellison was especially pleased to share the role of guest of honor at a dinner with T.S. Eliot, the poet whose work had affected Ellison so dramatically during his college days.

Ellison was among the few who were received by the Queen Mother and Princess Margaret, whom he referred to as "two very charming ladies indeed." (*Trading Twelves*, 143) He added that the Queen Mother was very conversant on literature (which surprised him).

On the return trip to Rome the Ellisons stopped in Munich, and in Germany both he and Fanny enjoyed walking the streets and discovering the beauty of the old city.

Through their correspondence and time spent together, the friendship between Ellison and Murray flourished during the years they were abroad. Much of their correspondence consisted of discussions about new cameras and camera equipment, including special lenses, light meters, and carrying cases. They also shared an intense love for jazz and often commented on artists and their latest recordings. No conversation about music was ever complete without a discussion of the latest recording equipment, including tape-recording machines which were becoming popular. Because the Murrays had access to the Post Exchange, they supplied the Ellisons with hard-to-get items such as Kleenex, Pond's cold cream, and most importantly, American coffee.

One other item of conversation that often came up was that of desegregation, which was just beginning to make inroads into American society during the fifties. The infamous 1957 attempt to desegregate the high school in Little Rock, Arkansas—reinforced by Federal troops—took place while Ellison was in Rome, and the incident upset him so that he could hardly write about it, even in a letter to his friend.

In the fall of 1956, Ellison received an invitation to be a member of the American delegation to the Mexico City Conference on Cultural Freedom in the Western Hemisphere. He planned to use the trip to make a stop in New York City, and check on the Harlem apartment.

Ellison disagreed in principle with much of what he saw and heard at the Mexico conference, but he enjoyed Mexico City, feeling it was every bit as fascinating as Rome. The return trip took him to Paris where a damp winter had set in with a vengeance, and after spending a few days there to report to the committee responsible for sending him to Mexico, he returned to Rome and to Fanny.

As Ellison's time in Rome was winding down, Fanny sailed for home on July 23, 1957. Because he was scheduled for a trip to Japan in September, it was decided that she should return to New York early.

That same summer Ellison received a visit from the granddaughter of J.D. Randolph, the man who'd been like a grandfather to him during his childhood. She was vacationing with her husband and son in the area, and they spent their time together reminiscing and recalling the jazz climate of Oklahoma City during their formative years. Randolph's granddaughter believed the musical achievements of those years were merely accidental, but Ellison insisted those musicians were highly conscious of what was happening. He explained the art of jazz and its use as a universal language, a subject he would explore to a greater extent in the coming years.

Following his fall trip to Japan (with stops in Hong Kong and Calcutta) Ellison returned to Rome to prepare to return home to the United States. He sailed for the United States on an Italian freighter arriving November 14, 1957. A few short months later, the Murrays were transferred to the Air Reserve Flying Center at Long Beach, California, placing both families stateside once again.

During his first few months in Rome, Ellison had received an invitation to take a position at Brandeis University, located ten miles outside of Boston, and teach courses in American Literature and creative writing. The offer was appealing to him because it was near Harvard in Cambridge; however, as the negotiations continued to unfold, the offer became less attractive and in the end he changed his mind and turned it down, taking a position at Bard College beginning in the spring of 1958.

Bard College with its six-hundred-acre campus, is located in Annandale-on-Hudson, New York, on the east bank of the Hudson River 90 miles north of New York City. Ellison taught American and Russian literature at the school until 1961.

During this time Ellison produced a number of essays on music and musicians. The first and best known was "The Golden Age, Time Past," published in *Esquire* in the spring issue, 1959 which traced the origin of bebop. Other articles were "The Charlie Christian Story," "Remembering Jimmy," and "As the Spirit Moves Mahalia."

Meanwhile, work on Ellison's second novel never stopped, although his attention to it was somewhat sporadic. New characters were developed and old characters expanded as he wrote, edited, and rewrote. By 1960, several episodes from the manuscript were edited into a sequence entitled "And Hickman Arrives." The piece was published in an issue of *Noble Savage*, a literary journal edited by Saul Bellow.

One feature of the plot involved a series of political assassinations and, when the assassinations of John F. Kennedy, Robert Kennedy, Malcolm X, and Martin Luther King Jr. actually took place, Ellison was forced to rethink the plot. "One of the things which really chilled me— slowed the writings—was the eruption of assassinations ... because suddenly life was stepping in and imposing itself upon my fiction." (Current Biography Yearbook, 1993)

As the sixties progressed, militant groups of young blacks criticized Ralph Ellison for not being more vocal and more active in the Civil Rights movement. Because he did not follow their lead in the "black is beautiful" mentality or endorse a return to African roots, he was labeled by students as an Uncle Tom. They felt Ellison did not display enough rage in his writing, but he retorted he was unable to view Africa as his homeland and could see no significant relationship between American blacks and Africans.

"The Africans I've met in Paris and Rome have seen me as an alien. They see most American Negroes this way.... I won't have anything to do with racial approaches to culture." (Graham, 64) Ellison believed being a Negro-American made him a member of an American cultural group and had very little to do with African culture. He longed for blacks in America to appreciate and understand their own true culture. "As long as Negroes are confused as to how they relate to American culture," he said, "they will be confused about their relationship to places like Africa." (Graham, 69) Ellison insisted that art is a celebration of human life rather than a wailing complaint about social wrongs.

In Ellison's eyes there was no such thing as a free-floating culture, and everything in America resulted from exchange and interplay. In his essays he pointed out that slaves on Southern plantations watched white people dance and then transformed those dance steps into something entirely their own. "He (Ellison) speaks of what Ella Fitzgerald has done with the songs of Rogers and Hart, what white rock bands did with the blues; he watches the black kids in Harlem in their baggy hip-hop gear walking down Broadway and on the same day he sees white suburban kids on television affecting the same style." (Graham, 396)

In a 1960 interview, Ellison stated "I recognize no American style in literature, in dance, in music, even in the assembly-line processes, which does not bear the mark of the American Negro." (Graham, 174) Because he could see so much good in black culture, it pained him to see blacks reducing their American experience to sheer victimization.

In 1964, Random House published his book of essays, reviews, and interviews, entitled *Shadow and Act*. The book explored the relationship between the Negro-American subculture and the North American culture and gave readers insight into the person behind the name Ralph Ellison.

THE FINAL YEARS

For many years, Ellison and Fanny had thought about purchasing a summer home, a respite from the city to enjoy peace and quiet. They finally found a 200-year-old house in the Berkshires of Pittsfield, Massachusetts and spent time and money renovating it and moving in the summer of 1967. One cold November day, they went shopping in town and when they returned they found the house engulfed in flames. The house was in a remote area and the local volunteer fire department was in another location fighting another fire, and by the time they arrived the house had burned to the ground. The Ellisons lost many prized possessions and mementos, but the most traumatic loss was the more than 360 pages of the second novel, of which there was no copy.

"Ralph was just devastated," noted his friend Al Murray. "He just closed in on himself for a long time. He didn't see anyone or go anywhere. At a certain point, you knew not to say much about it. A wall, Ralph's reserve, went up all around him." (Graham, 394)

All he could do was struggle to piece it back together again. "Let's say I was disoriented," he admitted, "but I worked on it. I don't know how long the interruption was. Maybe four or five years." (Graham, 395)

The fire proved to be a serious setback, but he continued to work on the book and by the next decade the manuscript measured over nineteen inches thick. By then, he had purchased a copier and all the pages were safely copied and stored.

As the years passed, honors and awards continued to come Ellison's way. In 1965, in a *Book Week* poll (the literary review supplement of the New York *Herald Tribune*), two hundred authors, editors, and critics selected *Invisible Man* as the most distinguished novel published by an American during the previous twenty years.

In 1968, he was made a *Chevalier de l'Ordre des Artes et Lettres,* one of the highest compliments that France can pay to a writer of foreign birth. Ironically, the presentation was made by author André Malraux, the Minister of Culture in France, and the man whose works were given to the young Ellison the first day he arrived in Harlem in 1936. During the following year, 1969, President Lyndon B. Johnson awarded Ralph Ellison the Medal of Freedom, America's highest civilian honor. Throughout the country's involvement in Vietnam, Ellison supported Johnson's war policy, which contributed to his unpopularity with young students protesting against the war.

Along with awards came honorary degrees for the Tuskegee "dropout." Ellison received honorary doctorates from Tuskegee,

Rutgers, Michigan, Williams, Harvard and Wesleyan. He was also awarded fellowships by the National Academy of Arts and Letters, and by Yale University. In 1975 the Ralph Ellison Public Library was dedicated in his honor in his hometown of Oklahoma City, Oklahoma.

During the years that television made its entrance into homes across the nation, Ellison took a vital interest in the medium. From the outset he believed strongly that television could be harnessed and used for education and enlightenment. He served for years on the Carnegie Commission on Educational Television, whose findings led to the formation of the Public Broadcasting Service. "The whole movement of the society," he stated, "is toward discovering who we are." (Graham, 388) Television, he believed, could be one of the primary forces in that discovery.

Among his many other roles in public service, he served on the board of the Kennedy Center for the Performing Arts in Washington D.C., and as a member of the American Academy-Institute of Arts and Letters.

Ellison's speaking skills were polished through the years until he was able to present a ninety-minute speech without the aid of notes. While he might make a few digressions to emphasize a certain point, he would deftly return to pick up the thread and move through to the end. By the early seventies, he was making 20 such appearances a year, mostly on the East Coast or in the Midwest.

For decades, Ellison and Fanny lived comfortably in an over-crowded one-bedroom apartment on the outer fringes of Harlem.

The old, once-grand apartment building was situated on a corner, and from his eighth-floor window he could look down upon the Hudson River, Riverside Drive, and the railroad tracks. From his window he also enjoyed one of his favorite pastimes—bird watching. As he moved about the apartment from room to room, his Labrador retriever, Tuckatarby, remained close by his side. The apartment was filled with an enormous collection of books and there were bookshelves everywhere. The desk in his study was hidden under mounds of papers, and stacks of neatly labeled file boxes lined the floor. It was Fanny's job to look after the boxes and his files. She could, Ralph boasted, find anything. Art objects and artifacts adorned the larger study and included Kachina dolls from the Hopi and Zuni Indians, and paintings, etchings, and photographs were tastefully hung on the walls.

His workday began each morning by six or seven. After breakfast he would write from nine in the morning until four in the afternoon. Through the years, he advanced from a typewriter, to an electric typewriter, and eventually to a computer. The only variation to his disciplined work schedule were those days when he taught classes at New York University. Evenings were spent with Fanny talking over his work, editing, and reading passages aloud. His wife had always been his first reader and in the early days she had often typed his manuscripts for him. Before retiring, Ellison and Tuckatarby took the apartment's decrepit elevator to the first floor to go outside for a late night walk.

In 1980, Ellison retired from his teaching duties as Schweitzer Professor of Humanities at New York University. Two years later, in 1982, Random House issued a special 30th anniversary edition of *Invisible Man*, which included an insightful introduction by the author. The Book-of-the-Month Club also distributed this edition. During the 30 years since its original publication, *Invisible Man* had gone through 20 hardcover and 17 Vintage Book paperback printings. Additionally, there was a Modern Library edition and by 1982, the novel could be read in Czech, Danish, Dutch, Finnish, French, German, Hebrew, Hungarian, Italian, Japanese, Norwegian, Portuguese, Slovak, Spanish, and Swedish.

Another book of essays, speeches, interviews, and reviews—many of them two decades old—was published in 1984 entitled *Profiles: Going to the Territory*. Ellison used the book as a platform to lend insight into his background and into jazz as well as jazz musicians.

Still there was no published second novel, although Ellison worked on it daily. In one interview, he quipped, "If I'm going to be remembered as a novelist, I'd better produce it soon." (Graham, 382)

For Ellison's eightieth birthday, Random House hosted a small dinner in his honor on the evening of March 1, 1994. Some friends were invited, one of whom was Albert Murray. The two traded toasts and responses, unaware it was the last time they would ever see one another. Six weeks later on April 16, 1994, Ellison succumbed to pancreatic cancer. He and Fanny had been married for forty-seven years.

Epilogue

Ralph Ellison spent decades reconstructing, revising, and expanding his initial vision of the much-discussed second novel. When he died in 1994, he left behind some 2,000 pages of manuscript; yet this mountain of prose was still unfinished. Hence, it was assumed that the second novel would never be published.

A year after Ellison's death, Fanny appointed John F. Callahan, the Morgan S. Odell Professor of Humanities at Lewis and Clark College, as literary executor. Callahan and Fanny together decided to edit the manuscript—which Callahan described as "multifarious, multifaceted, multifocused, multivoiced, and multitoned"—and publish the work. (*New York Times* 1) The first step, of course was cutting down the size and, pieces of the huge manuscript had to be quarried from all the raw material. It was an exhausting undertaking.

"Aiming, as Ellison had, at one complete volume," Callahan wrote, "I proceeded to arrange his oft-revised, sometimes reconceived scenes and episodes according to their most probable development and progression. While doing so, I felt uneasily Procrustean: Here and there limbs of the manuscript needed to be stretched, and elsewhere a protruding foot might be lopped off, if all the episodes were to be edited into a single, coherent, continuous work." (*New York Times* 1)

Fanny gave Callahan a free hand and he spent three years before he felt it was ready. He had known Ellison since the late 1970s, and when he wrote and published an essay about Ellison's work, he had received a friendly note from the author.

When Callahan became executor in 1995, he knew little about Ellison's second novel, other than the fact that Ellison had worked on it for a very long time, and that the author had been concerned about the "transitions" between the sections.

Callahan's version, entitled *Juneteenth*, appeared in 1999 to mixed reviews. Some contended that Ellison never intended for the book to be published, and there was no indication he'd chosen that title (for the work remained untitled for all the years he worked on it). Others felt the editing was choppy at best and weakened the work.

Ellison's original manuscript appeared to have at least three plot lines, a dozen or more different narrators, and a timeline that centered on the mid-1950s; it then spiraled back to the beginning of the century and looked forward to the tumultuous sixties. Gone were the epic proportions that Ellison so clearly envisioned—instead, *Juneteenth* revolved around just two characters. "Instead of the symphonic work Ellison envisioned," wrote Michiko Kakutani in a *New York Times* article, "Callahan has given us a single, tentatively rendered melodic line. Instead of a vast modernist epic about the black experience in America, he has given us a flawed linear novel, focused around one man's emotional and political evolution." (*New York Times* 1)

Whatever the fate of *Juneteenth*, nothing can ever detract from Ellison's *Invisible Man*—a book that is viewed as one of the most important works of fiction in the 20th century. His classic work has been read by millions, and has influenced dozens of younger writers; it established Ellison as one of history's major American writers. The book is now a standard work of American fiction in the nation's schools and colleges.

However fascinating and powerful, it is the man behind the book who contributed so much to society. Quietly, persistently, Ralph Ellison made his influence felt in the halls of the intellectual world both in the United States and abroad. In the face of opposition he remained true to the person he knew himself to be—not a man of color, but a man with a rich cultural heritage, and a man who felt a responsibility to that heritage.

While he never would accept the racial slurs and rebuffs he received from some critics, he learned to live above them. "I'm utterly amused when I go into a store to spend $100 and some little clerk is rude," he said. "You see, I don't allow anonymous people to give me my sense of worth." (Graham, 108)

WORKS CITED

Anderson, Jervis. "Going To The Territory." *The New Yorker* (November 22, 1976).

Ellison, Ralph. *Shadow and Act*. New York: Random House, 1964.

Busby, Mark. *Ralph Ellison*. New York: Twayne Publishers, 1991.

Graham, Maryemma and Amritjit Singh, eds. *Conversations With Ralph Ellison*. Jackson, Miss: University Press of Mississippi, 1995.

Inge, M. Thomas, Maurice Duke, Jackson R. Bryer, eds. *Black American Writers Vol. I*. New York: St. Martin's Press, 1978.

Inge, M. Thomas, Maurice Duke, Jackson R. Bryer, eds. *Black American Writers Vol. II.* New York: St. Martin's Press, 1978.

Kakutani, Michiko. "'Juneteenth': Executor Tidies Up Ellison's Unfinished Symphony." *The New York Times* (May 25, 1999).

Murray, Albert and John F. Callahan. *Trading Twelves.* New York: The Modern Library, 2000.

O'Meally, Robert G. *The Craft of Ralph Ellison.* Cambridge, Mass.: Harvard University Press, 1980.

THOMAS HEISE

Race, Writing, and Morality: Cultural Conversations in the Works of Ralph Ellison

In the summer of 1945 Ralph Waldo Ellison set up his typewriter in the open doorway of an old barn in Waitsfield, Vermont and typed out what was to become one of the most famous first lines in American literature: "I am an invisible man." He then paused while crumpling the page for the wastebasket. It was at this moment, as Ellison told it in 1980, "a shadow of the speaker arose in my mind and I grasped at his range of implication." Over the next seven years Ellison would stalk his Invisible Man from the South to the North, would try to track down the nebulous identity of his narrator as he slipped above and below the dark New York City streets, and would finally find him holed up beneath 1,369 lights in an underground apartment near Harlem—where the unnamed hero was himself writing—"trying to put it all down"—the book Ellison would finally publish in 1952 as *Invisible Man*. Ellison's years of work had finally paid off. Anthony West hailed *Invisible Man* in an early review in *The New Yorker* as "exceptionally good," a novel of "absolute authenticity," and proclaimed "[f]ew writers can have made a more commanding first appearance." With equal excitement, Webster Schott wrote in the *Kansas City Star* that Ellison's was "one of the best novels yet written by an American Negro." The committee for the National Book Award went further and honored Ellison's novel as the best of the year. In the years since its publication, the superlatives have continued to mount up. "[T]he most distinguished single work" published since World War II announced *Book Week* in a 1965 poll. The renowned literary critic Harold Bloom agrees, calling *Invisible Man* the

51

principal work of American fiction to be published between William Faulkner's major phase in the 1930s and Thomas Pynchon's 1973 opus *Gravity's Rainbow*. But as the years and decades passed, Ellison's audience grew impatient for a second novel, rumors of which had been circulating since shortly after the publication of *Invisible Man*. When over three hundred pages of that second novel were destroyed in a fire at Ellison's house in the 1960s, he began again. "There will be something very soon," Ellison promised in 1994, though in truth he had shown his publisher, Random House, nothing. Ellison died two months later, leaving his literary executor to cobble together the novel, *Juneteenth* (1999), from thousands of unorganized pages. Reviews were negative. Louis Menand's first reaction was "This is not Ralph Ellison's second novel." Despite this late second effort, a handful of short stories, two essay collections, *Shadow and Act* (1964) and *Going to the Territory* (1986), Ellison's indispensable place in the American literary canon rests almost entirely on the achievement of *Invisible Man*, the novel he liked to call "a struggle through illusion to reality," a fitting description of Ellison's own compositional difficulties.

When Ellison typed out *Invisible Man*'s famous first words he was depressed and sick with a kidney infection that he had contracted from contaminated water while serving on a Merchant Marine's ship during 1944's Battle of the Bulge. Perhaps Ellison's maritime experience led him to think of Herman Melville, whom he praises in *Shadow and Act* as a novelist who "took a moral responsibility for democracy" and who represented African Americans in a way that few had—"as a symbol of Man." Melville's preoccupation with the plight of extraordinary individuals under extraordinary pressures finds an analogue in Ellison's story of the trials and tribulations that Invisible Man must endure on his quest for identity, which Schott labels a "universal rather than a racial theme." But Ellison's aims were clearly national, not universal, when he selected Melville's *Benito Cereno* to serve as the epigraph for his novel about the distorted representation of African Americans by whites. In Melville's novella the Spaniard, Cereno, gradually becomes aware, in a way that his American counterpart Captain Delano does not, of the intelligence of Babo, the slave who has mutinied Cereno's vessel. Incapable of coping with the knowledge that "the black—whose brain, not body" had usurped his power, Cereno dies. The passage that Ellison presents at the opening of *Invisible Man* has Cereno on his deathbed next to an astonished Delano who questions him, "you are saved: what has cast such a shadow upon you?" Cereno's answer, which Ellison coyly leaves out, is "The Negro." Cereno's response effectively launches Ellison's exploration in *Invisible Man* of what it means for his African-American narrator to be "a shadow," "a phantom," to be a "figment of ... imagination" in the minds of white Americans.

Invisible Man originates with Ellison's postwar sickness and depression, conditions aligning him with the "melancholy" Cereno. To represent a slave as an intelligent being to an exclusively white readership was a risk for Melville in 1855. What Cereno could not cope with, became for Ellison a creative opportunity. In the introduction to the Thirtieth Anniversary Edition of his novel, Ellison reveals that his aim was "to create a narrator who could think as well as act," a goal that he found particularly pressing since "most protagonists of Afro-American fiction (not to mention the black characters in fiction written by whites) were without intellectual depth." For models of hyperconsciousness, Ellison looked from Melville to Henry James to provide examples of characters who could "snatch the victory of conscious perception." Throughout his writing career, he acknowledged his debt to other authors: Mark Twain, who taught him the importance of comedy as an antidote to the ailments of politics, Ernest Hemingway, whose use of understatement Ellison borrowed for some of his early short fiction, and T. S. Eliot and James Joyce, from whom Ellison learned to use archetypal patterns as a method for structuring experience in *Invisible Man*. To the student of literature, the narrator's initial, ironic declaration of identity echoes the declarative opening of *Moby Dick*, "Call me Ishmael." The reader of *Notes from Underground* will hear Ellison's narrator, who is literally in "a hole in the ground," parrot Dostoevsky's hero who introduces himself by claiming "I'm a sick man ... a mean man. I think there's something wrong with my liver." Given Ellison's kidney infection in 1945, the allusion reverberates on multiple levels. From its opening line to its final Whitmanian question—"Who knows but that, on lower frequencies, I speak for you?"—Ellison's rich novel shimmers with allusions to the world's most enduring literature.

To the list of Ellison's influences one should add Homer, Dante, Emerson, W. E. B. Du Bois, and Richard Wright, the jazz of Louis Armstrong, Duke Ellington, and Charlie Parker, stories from black folklore, (which Ellison overheard from the "older men [who] would sit with their pipes" in the drugstore where he once worked), African-American church sermons, Southern speech patterns, and a liberal dose of street slang. Unlike his High Modernist progenitors who eschewed popular culture for the classics, and unlike his fellow African-American novelists who wrote with a clear realistic prose, Ellison's work, as he states in *Going to the Territory*, brings together the "high" and the "low," the traditional and the popular, so as to "confound ... hierarchal expectations." In many respects *Invisible Man* is a straightforward critique of the American Dream, the reverse of the Horatio Alger story that asserts through hard work and determination one can rise through the rungs of American society. By the end of *Invisible Man*, the promising, upwardly mobile college student is a middle-aged man with a grudge, living in an abandoned apartment. Ellison has confounded our expectations, has aligned our sympathies with his "irresponsible" narrator. In part, he manages to do so by taking the reader along for Invisible Man's wild ride, starting from the terrifying battle royal where he receives his scholarship, to his adventure with the lunatics at the Golden Day, his expulsion from college, his near lobotomization by racist doctors, his stint with the Brotherhood (a thinly disguised version of New York's Communist Party), and finally through the hellish flames of Harlem's race riot. To cover this much territory, Ellison marshals all available resources, from Dante's mythic narrative of descent, to the syncopated rhythms of Louis Armstrong's jazz. What results is a story of vertigo: one man's experience of what Ellison called America's "cacophonic motion."

Invisible Man is a symphonic novel with echoing motifs and a mélange of styles. It is by turns naturalistic in its depiction of its narrator's struggle against forces threatening to contain him, symbolic with its repeating images of white and black, sight and blindness, freedom and claustrophobia, and surrealistic in episodes such as at the Golden Day where the narrator finds himself in a chaotic tavern peopled with mental patients, prostitutes, and a shell-shocked veteran prophesying "the end of the world." In his passages concerning the Brotherhood, Ellison employs a realistic mode of representation to lay bare the machinations of this corrupt political organization, while in the final, apocalyptic images of Harlem on fire, Ellison switches his register to a dreamlike prose that turns the burning world into a mirror for his narrator's internalized guilt. Through the shifting rhetoric emerges a story of maturation, a *bildungsroman* of a young black man whose life, Ellison says in his essays, is caught in the "fluid, pluralistic turbulence" of America. Speaking of his novel's various strategies of representation, Ellison reveals that he "dream[ed] of a prose which was flexible, and swift, confronting the inequalities and brutalities of our society forthrightly, but yet thrusting forth its images of hope, human fraternity and individual self-realization." Ellison is more than aware that the African-American experience in the highly segregated America of the 1930s and 1940s is often unreal and violent, and so it is indicative of the ongoing need to affirm, not reject, American ideals of justice and social equity. We should see Ellison's prose, with it's multiple strands of influence and wide-range of reference, as his democratic answer to the questions that the novel, he says in *Going to the Territory*, was designed to ask: "Who are we? What has the experience of the particular group been? How did it become this way? What is it that stopped us from attaining the ideal?"

Invisible Man attempts to answer these questions by focusing on the life of one representative individual—an allegorical Everyman, "a walking personification of the Negative." By his own admission in chapter one, Ellison's anonymous narrator is a "naïve" adolescent in search of an identity among the "quiet greenness" of his campus. He sheepishly admits, "I was looking for myself, and asking everyone except myself questions which I, and only I, could answer." Over the course of the novel he discovers his invisibility, a metaphor for the refusal of others—Dr. Bledsoe, Mr. Norton, members of the Brotherhood—to recognize his humanity and for his own failure to understand his desires. Images of blindness pepper the novel, from the scarf tied around his eyes prior to the boxing match in which he is forced to participate and held for an audience of whites at his graduation, to Homer Barbee's "sightless eyes," to Brother Jack's prosthetic that pops out during a heated political discussion. In each case, Invisible Man and the others suffer from limited vision, a failure to comprehend "the total American experience," by which Ellison means to convey something much more expansive than the Brotherhood's narrow ideology that promotes a politics of class at the expense of race. Identity, for Ellison's narrator, is not to be found by complying with the mandates of his college president, nor is it discovered in the structure of organized politics—though the Brotherhood literally gives him a new name. For Invisible Man it means integrating the black folk wisdom of Peter Wheatstraw and the irrepressible energy of Louis Armstrong with the ideals of the American flag, which have been perverted into a tattoo on a naked woman's belly. Through the hero's personal quest for a name he can call his own, Ellison's *Invisible Man* attempts to solve the American mystery of "Who are we" and "How did it become this way." Yet by the end, Ellison does not give us answers, but instead gives us better, more poignant questions: "[W]hat else could I do? What else but try to tell you what was really happening?"

Most reviews of *Invisible Man* published in the 1950s delighted in the breadth of its allusions, and took note of its reference to older epic forms recalled by its colorful episodic narrative. At a time of increasing racial tension in America, reviewers found reassurance in the apparently non-politicized answer to persistent problems of race and class in American culture. In other words, most of the initial critical assessments of *Invisible Man* complimented the novel as a richly textured, aesthetic object primarily concerned with the universal themes of maturation, betrayal, doubt, human mortality, all of which were woven together in the travails and travels of a modern *Pilgrim's Progress*. When addressing the novel's handling of how best to portray the experience of African-American life in a discriminatory society, Anthony West's response in *The New Yorker* was that *Invisible Man* is not "a grievance book," and was typical of the de-politicized atmosphere of the late 1940s and early 1950s, a time when "the end of ideology" was fast becoming a slogan among intellectuals and scholars who were increasingly dissatisfied with the solutions European and American politics offered to social ills. According to these criteria, novels like Ellison's were lauded for their artistic merits alone. We hear as much in West's elation that *Invisible Man* "has not got the whine of a hard-luck story about it, and it has not got the blurting, incoherent quality of a statement made in anger." What West applauds is the novel's rejection of organized politics and mass civil disobedience as answers to America's social ills, evidence for which is found in the narrator's rejection of all institutions of social, religious, educational, and political power. Invisible Man rebuffs these remedies because they process and program the individual for their own ends; he chooses, instead, to make his own way. Rather than a statement of anger, he makes a statement of love, eventually admitting to himself "I *have* to love" if he is ever going to leave his lair for the world above.

Ellison's novel is an unrepentant affirmation of American individualism, according to critics such as Anthony West, an assessment that finds support from Ellison himself. In the introduction to the 1982 edition of *Invisible Man*, he tells how he strenuously tried to "avoid writing what might turn out to be nothing more than another novel of racial protest instead of the dramatic study in comparative humanity." Ellison argues that novels, and especially his own, should not be mistaken for political propaganda, or as he asserts in *Shadow and Act*, they should not be judged according to whether they have the right presentation of "racial suffering, social injustice." *Invisible Man* is not a proposal to fix society—a point smartly conveyed by Peter Wheatstraw with his cart stuffed with discarded blueprints. With Wheatstraw's wisdom in mind, Invisible Man ultimately leaves the Brotherhood with Emma's words, "I can't believe that you're such an individualist," ringing in his ears. Like all of the other manipulative institutions he has passed through, the Brotherhood is a sign, he says, of "an increasing passion to make men conform to pattern." Both Ellison's satire of Communist orthodoxy and West's remark that it "is as moving and vivid a piece of writing on this difficult subject as one could wish to read," characterize writers and critics of the post-Stalin era, when ideologies posing total and final solutions were vigorously shunned. In Ellison's opinion, "all political parties are basically concerned with power and with maintaining power, not with humanitarian issues." When asked if his novel was a political protest, Ellison responded in earnest that "It protests the agonies of growing up." Its concerns are existential, not ideological. Eschewing organized dissent, Ellison always put his faith in the individual who confronts his or her "vulnerability before the larger forces of society and the universe" alone.

While it was widely applauded, *Invisible Man* did rouse dissenting voices in the 1950s, particularly among America's political Left. Some reviewers were skeptical of Ellison's refusal to advocate political engagement in his fiction; others were downright vitriolic. Abner W. Berry in *Daily Worker* writes off the novel as "439 pages of contempt for humanity, written in an affected, pretentious and otherworldly style to suit the kingpins of world white supremacy." John O. Killens reinforces that judgment in *Freedom* where he protests that "Negro people need Ralph Ellison's *Invisible Man* like we need a hole in the head." But perhaps the most important early negative appraisal of *Invisible Man* came in 1963 when Irving Howe in *A World More Attractive*, reprimanded Ellison's book for "the apparent freedom it displays from the ideological and emotional penalties suffered by Negroes in this country." Howe rebukes Ellison for succumbing to "the post-war *Zeitgeist*," particularly for his dismissal of organized politics—"[t]he middle section of Ellison's novel, dealing with the Harlem Communists, does not ring quite true," Howe states in contradistinction to West. Howe also rejects the narrator's assertion in the epilogue of his "unconditional freedom" in a "world ... of infinite possibilities," denouncing it as "vapid and insubstantial" and characteristic of "American literary people in the fifties." Howe's own comments in turn typify the politically charged early-1960s when America's civil rights movement was in full swing. Martin Luther King Jr. marched on Washington the same year Howe published his critique, and in the successive two years, the Civil Rights Act and the Voting Rights Act were passed in Congress. This is not to suggest that Ellison disapproved of these legislative milestones or of the civil disobedience that made them possible. Ellison and Howe parted company over the proper role of literature in a political world. Ellison was a product of his time, thought Howe—and Howe, for his part, was too.

In *A World More Attractive* Irving Howe charges Ellison with playing fast and loose with the penalties suffered by blacks in America, though in truth what he bristles against is Ellison's willingness to show his hero's suffering at the hands of other African Americans and his manhandling by a left-wing political organization (whose goals Howe, as a democratic socialist, supports.) Far from ignoring Invisible Man's suffering, Ellison's book might properly be called his chronicle of humiliation. When we first meet him in the prologue, he has already retreated underground as a result of years of mistreatment that began with the white business leaders who humiliate him even as they sponsor his matriculation to a college that closely resembles Ellison's Tuskegee. His life of abuse has only just begun. He is called a "Nigger" by his African-American college president; Invisible Man leaves for the North where, after his injury at Liberty Paints, he becomes the subject of frightening medical experiments. He then flees once again, this time into the arms of the Brotherhood that exploits him and the residents of Harlem in order to advance its narrow political agenda. Contrary to Howe, Invisible Man has suffered a great deal, and contrary to West, this novel is filled with ferocious anger as vividly portrayed in the dramatic opening episode when the narrator nearly knifes the unapologetic white pedestrian who bumps him. From his accrued experience of being invisible, the narrator learns to turn his condition into a weapon. He gains this enlightenment slowly on the rough road from innocence to experience. Lost and alone, displaced and dispossessed, the anonymous narrator asks early on "How had I come to this?" and laments, "I was losing ... the only identity I had ever known." By the novel's end, he at last comprehends the futility of his attempts to make his way in the world without first discovering the nature of his own self. Only by extracting himself from the manipulative agenda of others can he "think things out in peace, or, if not in peace, in quiet." Having been chased underground, Ellison's narrator resourcefully transforms his imperiled condition into an opportunity to learn new strategies for survival. "A hibernation is a covert preparation for more overt action," he announces from his makeshift foxhole that he keeps lit with stolen electricity. He has become his own powerbroker, confining the powerful Dr. Bledsoe, Mr. Norton, and Brother Jack to the ash heap of his past. Though he softens his anger by the time of the epilogue and realizes that he must fight *for* not *against* society, he remains adamant about protecting his fledgling individuality and is suspicious of any social institution (regardless of its goals) that demands conformity as a condition of membership.

Irving Howe's and Anthony West's reactions to *Invisible Man* form the two poles that framed much of the early critical debates of Ellison's novel. Howe, like many politicized critics of the 1960s, favored Richard Wright's 1940 social realist novel *Native Son* over Ellison's more stylistically experimental effort. Wright's exacting and detailed representation of the racist forces operating in American society has a clarity to it that resembles, for some critics, the objectivity of the social sciences. Wright's *Native Son*, Howe contends, could teach its readers about the oppressive mechanisms at work in their culture. Ellison's novel, with its bewildering surrealism and its loyalty to the rare individual, was much less useful as a piece of political pedagogy.

"Wright was overcommitted to ideology," Ellison said in a 1961 interview, though he was quick to add, "I, too, wanted many of the same things for our people." Over time Ellison carved out more and more distance from Richard Wright, who mentored Ellison during his early days in New York. In "The World and the Jug," an important essay included in *Shadow*, he fired back at Howe's charges that he lacked political and racial integrity and took exception with what Wright termed "'the essential bleakness of black life in America.'" Ellison's more generous view emphasized the full diversity, fluidity, wonder, and challenge of the African American experience, ingredients that mix with "an American Negro tradition which teaches one to deflect racial provocation and to master and control pain." In *Invisible Man*, Ellison does not "deny the harshness of existence," and at the same time he proudly affirms the dignity of his narrator's decision "to deal with it as men at their best have always done," which in Invisible Man's own words entails that one "continu[es] to play in face of certain defeat."

The diversity and wonder that Ellison speaks of in "The World and the Jug" are fully displayed in the mysterious character Rinehart in *Invisible Man*, whom the narrator finds himself impersonating when he dons a disguise of a hat and sunglasses while trying to escape a scuffle in Harlem. "Rine the runner and Rine the gambler and Rine the briber and ... lover and ... Reverend," Rinehart is both everyone and no one— nothing more than a matrix of different hats and differing personalities. He is rind and heart, surface and depth, both 'either' and 'or,' and is key to enabling Invisible Man to understand the possibilities of identity. Though he never materializes in the novel, he is, ironically, its supreme individualist. Everywhere Invisible Man turns he is mistaken for this protean character, leading him to question, "If dark glasses and a white hat could blot out my identity so quickly, who actually was who?" From Rinehart's example, Invisible Man learns the potential that inheres in an identity that shifts, lies, swirls, and disappears. Much like Ellison's refusal to be pigeonholed as a writer, Rinehart resists categorization. Like Wheatstraw, Rinehart is an antinomian figure, a trickster from African-American folklore who collapses hierarchies of authority and power, deflating egos in the process. He is also indicative, Ellison writes in one of his essays, of "America and change." Far from being "bleak," Rinehart's America is a place brimming with promise, "a beautiful absurdity" where "change [is] so swift and continuous *and intentional*."

Rejecting Howe's and Wright's characterization of black life in America, Ellison attuned himself to its cultural complexity and fluidity, evident not only in the character of Rinehart, but in the range of sources—classic American literature, jazz, regional dialects, black nationalism, and urban hustling—that he drew upon when crafting his dazzling, cacophonous novel of possibility.

For the hero in search of his own name, Rinehart is not only a source of enthrallment, but is, perhaps surprisingly, a cause for depression. Contemplating Rinehart's ability to remake himself *ad nauseam*, Invisible Man remarks, "The notion was frightening." While Rinehart symbolizes an unfettered freedom beyond the domains of any confining institution, he also represents what Tony Tanner calls in *City of Words* (1971), a terrifying chaos, an "utterly shapeless confusion" that "offers no opportunities for self-development or self-discovery." Tanner is keenly attuned to the complex dialectic in Ellison's novel, noting that constrictive social structures also help shape one's identity by "giv[ing] the individual an important role" to play. Ellison's narrator rejects those who attempt to mold him for their own ends, and he dismisses Rinehart's ubiquity as an empty mirage of freedom: "I caught a brief glimpse of the possibilities posed by Rinehart's multiple personalities," he says, "and turned away." Between these two extremes, the narrator charts a middle path and discovers "what many American heroes have discovered, that he is not free to reorganize and order the world, but he can at least exercise the freedom to arrange and name his perceptions of the world." As Tanner concludes, "His most important affirmation may be, not of any pattern in the outside world, but of the patterning power of his own mind." Of essence here is "pattern," a blueprint of the imagination, which Rinehart lacks. When Invisible Man hunkers down to write the story of his experience, he maps his mind and his anger with words. It's a bulwark against Rinehartian chaos and the Party's rigidity. The words are his, written on his terms alone.

In many respects, Tony Tanner's 1971 reading of *Invisible Man* has much in common with previous de-politicized approaches that stress the narrator's final withdrawal into his own mind, as opposed to focusing on the novel's dramatic action, which illustrates the narrator's confrontation with the world at large. In order to resuscitate political engagements, which were on the wane after the 1960s, Jerry Gafio Watts's 1994 study, *Heroism and the Black Intellectual*, seeks "to bring politics back into the discussion of Ellison and to do so without subjecting him to dogmatic ideological formulations." Watts achieves his aim by dialoguing Ellison with Irving Howe and Harold Cruse, whose 1967 polemic, *The Crisis of the Negro Intellectual*, sought "to valorize a version of black nationalism as the correct ideology of the black intellectual." A staunch believer in the melting pot theory of American citizenship, Ellison repudiated the appeals in the 1960s for a separate black culture and identity. The *Invisible Man*'s Ras the Destroyer, who loosely resembles the West Indian activist Marcus Garvey, is Ellison's rendering of the militant, black separatist, and embodies the character West terms an "anti-Communist and anti-white agitator." Ras represents an alternative to the corrupt Brotherhood as he calls for a brotherhood based on skin color, not political ideology. Trying to win over the narrator's colleague Clifton, Ras affirms, "We sons of Mama Africa, you done forgot? You black, BLACK!" and moments later appeals, "It took a billion gallons of black blood to make you.... So why don't you recognize your black duty, mahn, and come jine us." For his part, the narrator snubs Ras's pleas, eventually battles him, and then turns his back on the Brotherhood that has pitted these two black men against each other. According to Watts, this narrative development makes Invisible Man "nothing less than heroic." While Watts seeks to reinvigorate political readings of Ellison's novel, he sees it as transcending ideological affiliations. Ellison's narrator is an African-American version of the Nietzschean superman, or as Watts says, a human being "forged out an act of will."

In a similar vein to Jerry Gafio Watts, Richard Kostelanetz's *Politics in the African-American Novel* (1991) outlines the manner in which Ralph Ellison and other African-American authors offer up a "scathing and thorough critique ... of the standard political solutions for bettering Afro-American life." Kostelanetz follows Ellison's hero from his valedictory address, where he speaks of the need for "cultivating friendly relations with the Southern white man," to his Brotherhood orations, where he tries to enlist Harlem's residents in class struggle. Kostelanetz posits "the narrator confronts a succession of possible choices for Afro-Americans," all of them unsatisfying. While Watts historicizes Ras's black separatism, Kostelanetz's book traces the narrator's high school speech to Booker T. Washington's influential (though largely discredited) rhetoric of racial uplift in *Up from Slavery*

(1901). In Washington's words "[t]he whole future of the Negro rested largely upon the question as to whether or not he should make himself ... of such undeniable value to the community in which he lived that the community could not dispense with his presence." As the founder of Tuskegee, Washington believed that black self-improvement alone could ameliorate racial tension. In practice his ideas were too often predicated on African-American humility and too often let white racism off the hook. *Invisible Man*'s fictionalized version of Tuskegee portrays its leadership as secretly and selfishly obsessed with its own power while it publicly promotes a benign ethic of hard work. Invisible Man rejects it for the Brotherhood's more overt politics, only to find their demands for doctrinal obedience equally stultifying. As Kostelanetz argues, this radical movement understands neither the narrator nor his people, as evinced by how quickly they move him out of his room in Harlem and how they later undermine his efforts to help that besieged community. "Black and white, white and black.... Must we listen to this racist nonsense?" Tobitt, one the Party's leaders shouts, insensitive to the problems mounting on each side of the color line. *Invisible Man* is organized around three main political ideologies—Washingtonian accommodation, Communist class struggle, and militant black separatism—all of which fail to consider the plight of the impoverished people of Harlem or of the narrator, who finds himself enmeshed in society's "simple yet confoundingly complex arrangement of hope and desire, fear and hate."

Amidst a din of ideological pronouncements, the narrator's struggle to locate his own voice can be tracked by the numerous speeches he gives throughout the novel. If his graduation address finds him, as Kostelanetz suggests, innocently believing in the munificence of whites, then his work with the Brotherhood shows his indoctrination in the tenet that "the necessity of the historical situation" outweighs the needs of individuals. This doctrine is abandoned as he hears the first inklings of his own voice late in the novel during his eulogy for Tod Clifton. Having seen only faceless masses in prior speeches, he finally recognizes the "faces of individual men and women." He honors Clifton as a man not an ideologue, though he reprimands himself for failing to "bring in the political issues." In truth, Invisible Man has succeeded. By burying a part of his former self, he has learned to see others, even if they cannot see him, and has paved the way for his

discovery of his own voice, although it will take him until the epilogue
to speak clearly and directly. In Ellison's novel "[t]he end was in the
beginning" and so in the final pages, we meet once more the man from
the prologue who has said goodbye to the world in disgust. He has
abandoned the solutions of Bledsoe, Jack, and Ras in hopes of going
underground to nurse his wounds in peace. But as Kostelanetz argues,
"this solution too is inadequate." For Ellison, the artist should not
isolate himself for too long. As he writes in *Going to the Territory*, the
artist must engage the world "through the agency of mere words" in
order to give us a "sense of the human condition" in "volatile and
eloquent ways." The narrator concurs. On the brink of his ascension,
the harrowed narrator admits, "that even an invisible man has a socially
responsible role to play."

For Ellison, social responsibility was enacted through writing—
through "mere words." In an interview in *Shadow and Act*, he says the
African-American writer's "role is that of preserving in art those human
values which can endure by confronting change," even in the face of
"the obstacles and meannesses imposed upon us." Or as he has said
elsewhere, fiction is an "as if," a hypothetical gesture toward human
potential, that if taken seriously, holds the "potential for effecting
change." *Invisible Man* is a novel about confronting change. And it is a
book about how one endures in the face of seemingly insurmountable
obstacles. "[C]lubbed into [his] cellar," Invisible Man eventually
recognizes the futility of lashing back in anger. By the epilogue, the
prologue's outrage and energy is channeled into chronicling the
experience of his invisibility "in black and white." The narrator
transforms the simmering tensions and flares of violence between
blacks and whites into the black and white of the printed pages the
reader holds in his hands.

Throughout his journey toward maturation Invisible Man travels
farther and farther from his southern heritage until the very things that
bring pleasure like the sweet yams he devours from a street vendor—are
the source of "the greatest humiliation" and racial stereotypes. "You
have to leave home to find home," Ellison once scribbled in the margins
of a working draft of his novel. Writing is what brings the narrator
home, returns him to the world of the imagination, which Ellison
describes as a realm where "all people and their ambitions and interests
could meet." He has been told repeatedly to deny his past and his name

so that for much of his young life Invisible Man is not the author of his own experience. At each stage of the narrative, someone hands him another piece of paper, a high school diploma, Dr. Bledsoe's letters of recommendation, a slip of paper with his new Brotherhood name on it, but each of them hold another's black and white words, and all of them have instructions to "Keep This Nigger-Boy Running." He keeps them close in his briefcase and when he is chased into a pitch-black manhole during the Harlem riot, he burns the papers for light, thus, symbolizing that he will write his own way back to the surface. Though this collection of documents testifies to the manner in which he has been manipulated, it is not thrown away, but instead he uses it as a literal and figurative source of enlightenment. It is a signpost on his journey to self-discovery. Not only must he write his own future, but he also must learn to read, as Tanner says, the patterns of his past. Only after suffering brutality after brutality does he finally realize that his "past humiliations ... were more than separate experiences. They were me; they defined me.... and no blind men ... could take that, or change one single itch, taunt, laugh, cry, scar, ache, rage or pain of it."

Pain and happiness—these are the axes around which all of Ellison's work pivots. In *Shadow and Act*, a collection dedicated to the full range of African-American experience from the vexing poverty of Harlem in the 1940s to the brilliant saxophone of Charlie Parker, he details the proper function of the novel. "[T]rue novels," he postulates, "even when most pessimistic and bitter, arise out of an impulse to celebrate human life.... [T]hey would preserve as they destroy, affirm as they reject." "[T]he American novel had long concerned itself" with a mysterious fusion of peoples and cultures that Ellison calls "the puzzle of the one-and-the-many," words which might just as easily be attributed to the wily narrator of *Invisible Man*, who says "Our fate is to become one, and yet many" and then adds, "This is not prophecy, but description." While fascinated with the dynamism of American cultural pluralism, Ellison is no Pollyanna. The American experience may be filled with joy, but he also recognizes that it is replete with bitter rage. We are to accept and reject, much like Ellison's titular hero, who destroys the contents of his briefcase—a paper trail of deceit and exclusion—and yet he believes we are to stand by "the principle on which the country was built and not the men, or at least not the men who did the violence." With this epiphany, *Invisible Man* concludes:

violence begets violence; better the pen than the sword, better ink than blood.

In addition to further illuminating *Invisible Man*'s themes, Ellison's two essay collections, *Shadow and Act* and *Going to the Territory*, are important statements on American literature, race relations, jazz, the blues, democracy, morality, and lend insight into his own remarkable life story. Pulitzer-Prize-winning scholar R.W.B. Lewis treated *Shadow and Act* as "Ellison's real autobiography," to be distinguished from "the symbolic version given in his splendid novel of 1952." Much about Ellison's biography can be gleaned from his essays and his fiction. His early years as a music major at Tuskegee in Alabama and his eventual journey to New York, where he briefly associated with the city's Communist Party, find parallels in Invisible Man's northward migration, his stint with the Brotherhood, and his appreciation of Louis Armstrong, who "made poetry out of being invisible." In interviews titled "That Same Pain, That Same Pleasure" and "Some Questions and Some Answers" and in the autobiographical essay "Hidden Name and Complex Fate" we are invited into Ellison's past, but in each instance he urges us to view his experiences as representative of an African American "an unease of spirit" that emerges from the contradiction between America's "noble ideals and the actualities of our conduct." While Lewis highlights the autobiographical elements of Ellison's nonfiction, critic Stanley Edgar Hyman recognizes its visionary aspects, noting Ellison's exploration of the nationally and culturally resonant issues of race, frontier history, and the importance of ritual. Crowning Ellison "the profoundest cultural critic that we have," Hyman laments, "his hard doctrine of freedom, responsibility, and fraternity is a wisdom rare in our time."

Almost all of the interviews, essays, and speeches included in *Shadow and Act* elaborate on the ingredients of this three-part doctrine. In this 1964 collection and throughout his writing Ellison offers an image of America as a complex, integrated multicultural society where freedom and responsibility must be counted as necessary attributes of a national brotherhood that is flexible and forgiving in ways *Invisible Man*'s Brotherhood is not. Given the separatist rhetoric of Irving Howe, Harold Cruse, and Amiri Baraka, Ellison's vision of fraternity was indeed rare for the 1960s. As he argues in *Shadow*, the African American is inextricable from the American. "[T]he American Negro people is

North American in origin and has evolved under specifically American conditions," Ellison declares, noting that it draws its character from American slavery, emancipation, discrimination, all of which exist in a nation with "an explicitly stated equalitarian concept of freedom." While the Brotherhood's Tobitt believes he can choose to turn a deaf ear to America's black and white dialogue, Ellison thinks that choice is nonsensical since the two cultures share, among other things, a common history, language, and system of political representation. They are so tightly intermingled and intermarried that the two cultures have melted into one, diversity within unity.

As a student and composer of music, Ellison is particularly concerned with the health of American cultural production, especially as it addresses or ignores "the mystery of how each of us," despite our diversity, "is, nevertheless, American." In *Shadow*'s essay "Twentieth-Century Fiction," he chastises much of the literature written since 1900, accusing it of a thinness that stems from its stingy vision of American multiplicity and its essentially private nature. Twentieth-century novelists, in Ellison's purview, regularly shirk their commitment to the world around them, using bare-bones prose to explore questions of personal and psychological (rather than national and cultural) import. In contrast, nineteenth-century writers, such as Melville and Twain, blended personal stories with universal mythologies to create large, social novels that "managed to be about democracy." And to highlight the differences even further, Ellison remarks "After Twain's compelling images of black and white fraternity[,] the Negro as a rounded human being generally disappears from fiction." Instead he is replaced too frequently in twentieth-century literature with stereotypes and scapegoats that are symptomatic of "the unorganized, irrational forces of American life." Unwilling or unable to apprehend, he writes, "the complex experience which ceaselessly unfolds within this great nation," the modern novel stoically accepts the conditions of life. In short, it fails to lodge an imaginative protest. Disappointed with the "social irresponsibility" of the modern novel, Ellison finds sustenance from America's musicians. In "Living with Music," he discloses that he learned discipline from the jazz players he watched while growing up in Oklahoma. Inventive and swift, with a keen sense of tradition, jazz possesses the versatility that much twentieth-century literature lacks. More than just music, as Ellison-scholar Berndt Ostendorf contends, it is "a pervasive cultural style." "A marvel of social organization" is how Ellison describes a jam session, though he could have as easily been talking about another favorite subject, the ideal fluidity of American cultural democracy. He applauds the jazz circle's delicate balance "between strong individuality and the group" and offers it as model for the harmonic cultural pluralism for which America strives.

The essays in *Shadow* make it clear that Ellison's love of jazz was a love of America re-written in musical notes. As a young man, Ralph Ellison "terrorized a good part" of his hometown with imitations of Louis Armstrong's rowdy trumpet solos. The older Ellison we meet in "The Charlie Christian Story," has put down his trumpet, but still knows that jazz is not just America's only indigenous art form, but is a metaphor for its impromptu origins. African Americans have always felt the need to experiment, have always improvised their culture, recreating themselves when no viable images of them existed in the culture. In much the same vein, "jazz finds its very life in an endless improvisation," Ellison says, and then states, "the jazzman must lose his identity even as he finds it." In *Invisible Man* improvisation is a strategy for survival, for coping with one's invisibility, for "shaking off the old skin" and beginning anew. Beneath the 1,369 garish light bulbs in his re-wired apartment, the narrator imagines himself "in the great American tradition of tinkers," adding himself to the list of "Ford, Edison, and Franklin," though his closest kin is Louis Armstrong, whose song "What Did I Do to Be so Black and Blue" poses the question that drives this novel. Armstrong has bent his "military instrument into a beam of lyrical sound," into a beautiful weapon that makes music out of black and blue bruises. Armstrong's trumpet call has "demanded action" from Invisible Man, has demanded that he "play" responsibly. From jazz syncopation, he learns how to move: "Not only could you travel upward toward success but you could travel downward as well; up *and* down, in retreat as well as in advance, crabways and around in a circle." For the reader, Ellison's hero "play[s] the invisible music of [his] isolation," an improvisation that bends a life of discrimination into a triumphant song.

Ellison's fascination with jazz's fluid and spontaneous nature carried over into *Going to the Territory*, published twenty-two years after *Shadow*, making it the last work to appear before his death in 1994.

Ellison makes music the subject of the essays "The Little Man at Chehaw Station" and "Homage to Duke Ellington on His Birthday," but the collection resonates with many of the familiar themes heard in *Invisible Man* and *Shadow*: the purpose of the novel, the American compulsion for cultural invention, the dynamic and creative tension between blacks and whites and between the individual and society. Sounding much like Stanley Edgar Hyman, the novelist John Edgar Wideman also finds Ellison's voice in *Going* "assured, calm, wise." The literary critic Mark Busby agrees, labeling Ellison's second essay collection the work of "the elder statesman ... late in his career."

The essay "The Little Man at Chehaw Station," along with the two literary pieces, "Society, Morality, and the Novel" and "The Novel as a Function of Democracy," are Ellison's final defense of the traditional, but fast-eroding image of America as a melting pot. In "The Little Man" he laments, "Today that metaphor is noisily rejected, vehemently disavowed." In the face of "glaring inequities, unfulfilled promises, and rich possibilities of democracy," Americans have abandoned their faith in cultural integration and have replaced it with "the newly fashionable code word 'ethnicity.'" What stirs Ellison to anger is proprietary claims to culture made by the likes of *Invisible Man*'s Ras, in the name of "ancestral blood." As Morris Dickstein argues, Ellison's writing is a "classically pluralist defense of cultural diversity." Ellison's conviction was that America's entire cultural heritage was raw material for the artist to bend into "a beam of lyrical sound." The artist is morally obligated to make music from America's clash of cultures, or as Ellison writes in "Society, Morality, and the Novel," our national literature must "seiz[e] from the flux and flow of our daily lives those abiding patterns of experience" from which we form our sense of humanity and our sense of the humane. Unfortunately, Ellison's survey of American literature in his 1967 essay, "The Novel as a Function of American Democracy," like his earlier piece in *Shadow*, finds few reasons to rejoice. Instead of a vision of cultural diversity, the contemporary novel is "a cry of despair." Disappointed but ever patient, he again turns back to the rich work of Mark Twain, Henry James, and Stephen Crane for inspiration.

Ellison's novel and two essay collections often overlap, each expressing his disappointment, optimism, and sense of responsibility—a moral triptych. Invisible Man paints on the sky when he looks up and announces that "Sometimes I feel the need to reaffirm all of it, the whole unhappy territory." *Going to the Territory* and *Shadow and Act* are, in the end, reaffirmations of a national and personal identity founded on the eloquent mastery and control of pain. In his essays, Ellison reflects upon how one might stake out a course of action to shore up an artistic response against the aching uncertainties of existence. In his novel, we see him transform these theoretical concerns into the dramatic life journey of his young, easily bamboozled Everyman. They are themes that he was only capable of mastering after testing them in the short fiction he published in journals during the 1940s. Long unavailable except in their original venues, these stories, along with a number of unpublished others, were culled together two years after his death by his literary executor, John Callahan, and released as *Flying Home and Other Stories* (1996). Though freestanding and complete, the stories in *Flying Home* are, in Callahan's words, partial maps that "led Ralph Ellison into the territory of the novel—toward *Invisible Man*, with its freighted, frightening, fraternal 'lower frequencies' of democracy."

Ellison made his way into that territory slowly, crafting and refining the look of his Invisible Man in the stories "King of the Bingo Game" and "Hymie's Bull" where down-and-out characters chart their footsteps through a world full of racist violence, fatigue, and moments of surprising tenderness. With no name, no birth certificate, and no money, the protagonist of "King of the Bingo Game" is practically invisible. When he has a chance to win a bingo jackpot, he balks out of fear, refuses to stop the wheel from turning, and in a moment of dizzying, visionary wonder asks "Who am I?," the same question that Invisible Man poses as he regains consciousness in the post-explosion aftermath at Liberty Paints. Similarly, in "Hymie's Bull" Ellison puts his title character through a series of extreme experiences to test his responses for grace under pressure. Forced to kill a bull with only a knife in his hand, Hymie is a poor man's version of Hemingway's noble Spanish matador. As Hymie drives in his knife, Ellison drives home his theme—control or risk being controlled, a lesson that his counterpart, Invisible Man, recognizes in the paintings of bullfights hanging behind the one-eyed Jack at El Toro Bar. Hymie's story concludes with him lighting out at night from Alabama on a train heading toward sunrise, much like Invisible Man who, having been tested and enlightened, is poised to rise once again into daylight.

In *Flying Home* Ellison draws upon his literary influences and his personal history to craft short narratives that, as in *Invisible Man*, are evidence of his stylistic range and restlessness. The opening story, "A Party Down at the Square," is a tour-de-force written in a tough, reticent prose that, like the imagery in "Hymie's Bull," owes its debt to Hemingway. Its young, unnamed, white narrator witnesses men who are known as upstanding members of the community set fire to a helpless black man. The narrator fights to maintain his cool, though he soon succumbs to a visceral sickness, which suggests that on the inside he is, like Hemingway's Lieutenant Henry, roiling with disgust and latent anger. As he does in "Hymie's Bull," Ellison makes use of his experience riding the rails from Oklahoma to Alabama in "I Did Not Learn Their Names." "[O]n the road you really had no place," remarks the freight-hopping protagonist. The sentiment echoes of unfettered freedom laced with sadness and a touch of loneliness that anticipates Invisible Man's isolation. As Callahan has pointed out, the story "moves in the syncopated rhythms of the freights its narrator rides." Like its prose, it is a story of rough riding, written with a symbolic realism Ellison will perfect with the punishing boxing match that opens his novel.

Of the thirteen stories collected in *Flying Home*, the title story, published just a year before Ellison initiated work on *Invisible Man*, remains his most fully realized early treatment of what, in retrospect, has emerged as two of his enduring concerns: the pursuit of black self-improvement in the face of systemic white racism and the importance of "home," here figured as the traditions of Southern black folklore, to the hero questing for identity. The story of an African-American pilot from the North who crashes in a white man's field in Alabama, weaves an intricate meditation on human aspiration and arrogance that Ellison offers in both mythic and realistic terms. The historical impetus for "Flying Home," explains Susan Blake in "Ritual and Rationalization," is the scandal surrounding Tuskegee's air school, which was "established during World War II in response to complaints about discrimination against blacks in pilot training," but which "trained black men to fly but never graduated them to combat." The injured pilot Todd, has tried to best this bigotry, yet in his attempt he makes apparent his own prejudices. Jefferson, a poor, black sharecropper who waits with him until help arrives, queries him on why he wants to fly, to which Todd haughtily replies, "Because it makes me less like you."

As in the case of the mythical Icarus, Todd's hubris sends him tailspinning to earth where he must discover the value of folk wisdom as a stabilizing force. Todd's is a narrative of descent; he is brought down to the South to listen to Jefferson who is Ellison's version of Shakespeare's wise fool—a Falstaff who speaks truth through laughter. Despite personal experience with the effects of racial discrimination, Todd pledges his allegiance to the white-run military establishment instead of the old "peasant" who aides him after his plane hits a soaring buzzard, a scavenger that Ellison aligns with "jimcrows," a pun on the Jim Crow laws that maintained Southern racial segregation. While they wait for medical help, Jefferson spins a yarn about buzzards feasting on a sick horse that resembles the immobile Todd splayed out in a field. If Todd is attentive, he will recognize that in Jefferson's story, he is the victim of both white discrimination and his own black self-hatred. Jefferson follows with a tall tale relating how he managed to fly faster and more deftly than anyone in heaven, even when Saint Peter tried to clip his wings and strap a harness to him. It is Jefferson's chance to one-up Todd and his high-flying antics, but more importantly, it thematizes the uncontainable vigor of black folk wisdom. The moral of Ellison's story is that Todd should not be tethered to his ancestral blood at home. Rather, he must integrate his black roots into all his flights of the human spirit, a point conveyed by an exchange where Jefferson admonishes him, "'You black, son,'" and then adds, "'You have to come to the white folks, too.'" These are words that make Todd feel "at once consoled and accused." By the end, Todd is "lifted out of his isolation," carried off the farm and "back into the world of men," conscious that during his next flight he'll rise remade, "a dark bird" that also glows like "flaming gold."

With "Flying Home" and *Invisible Man* Ellison takes the archetypal story of descent and rebirth and reworks it showing the pressures of discrimination against the African American. But the stories also reflect tales of side-by-side communication. Todd learns to listen and respond to Jefferson, and in a manner that is not entirely different, Invisible Man negotiates an inner dialogue that by the novel's last line allows him to glance at his reader and ask if "I speak for you?" In Ellison's works, conversations are rarely easy, perhaps because they are metaphors for larger, national conversations covering race, culture, and history. In both *Invisible Man* and his short stories Ellison pursues this premise, but it is not until *Juneteenth*, his forty-year-in-the-making, unfinished epic novel, that he finds room to expound upon it fully.

The circumstances surrounding the publication of *Juneteenth* (1999) have stirred much critical ire, though most of it has been directed not at Ellison, but at his editor John Callahan, who stitched together the book from 2,000 pages of notes, printouts, and incomplete paragraphs and reduced and rearranged Ellison's original plan for a novel to be published in three volumes into what Callahan labels "a single, coherent, continuous work." The critic Michiko Kakutani takes exception to Callahan's characterization and sees *Juneteenth* as "disappointingly provisional and incomplete," and not surprisingly "opaque" given that Callahan "has effectively changed the book's entire structure and modus operandi." Reviewing it for *The New York Times*, Louis Menand is even more straightforward, stating "It seems unfair to Ellison to review a novel he did not write." Of course Ellison did write *Juneteenth*, though he did not finish it, nor did he leave anyone instructions for arranging it. These questions aside, what Callahan has made of the work Ellison left behind is a novel about the bedside conversation between an African-American revivalist preacher named Reverend Hickman and his adopted white racist son, Senator Sunraider. Sunraider languishes from an assassination attempt related at the novel's opening in the early 1950s, and is a Promethean figure rising from humble origins who, like Todd, turns his back on his heritage and rejects his father's name only to ask of him years later "Are you still here?" At times, talking to each other, at times, talking at cross-purposes, and at many times lost in their own reveries, father and son slowly reveal the personal and national histories that transpired during their long separation.

In one of *Juneteenth*'s most memorable flashbacks, the give and take of conversation is transformed into the call-and-response sermon delivered by Hickman and young Sunraider (then named Bliss) to commemorate Juneteenth, or June 19, 1865, a date celebrating slavery's end. Searching for a lost paternal intimacy from the past, Hickman says to his ailing and estranged son, "Bliss, we preached and you were with us through it all. You were there, boy." Capturing the moment's drama, Ellison writes "The Senator lay listening, feeling the pain rise to him again as he tried to surrender himself to the mellow evocation of the voice become so resonant now with pleasure and affirmation."

Sunraider's pain is physical and spiritual; he has sinned, and like the prodigal son, has returned. For much of *Juneteenth* the race-baiting Sunraider remains an unpleasant and mysterious character, his motivations hard to parse from Ellison's incomplete saga. But in this quiet bedside moment he is humanized, his conscience pained, as he becomes aware that his father's generous voice is filled with an affirmation of life that epitomizes Ellison's characters at their best. Throughout Ellison's posthumous novel Sunraider drifts in and out of consciousness, occasionally glimpsing the "victory of conscious perception," and always waking to find his father, the book's source of moral integrity, is still there. Four and a half decades after *Invisible Man*'s epigraph, Ellison completes Cereno and Delano's dialogue on race. Sunraider still has a shadow cast upon him, but it is his father's, and so, is shaped like his own.

Along with *Juneteenth*, what holds Ellison's short stories, essays, and *Invisible Man* together is an unwavering commitment to "conscious thought." The kinship between each of his embattled protagonists may be indexed by their shared skin color, but for Ellison this is only a superficial indicator. More significantly, they are survivors of initiatory experiences that awaken them to the damning effects of power and to the possibility of harnessing it in less damaging ways. Ellison's characters shed their naïve illusions or these are shredded for them, and surface from their experiences leaner, skeptical, scarred, a little scared, but not disillusioned. Invisible Man steals from Monopolated Light & Power as a way of feeling a "vital aliveness" that illuminates him in his darkest moment. "I can hear you say, 'What a horrible, irresponsible bastard!'" exclaims the narrator in hopes of anticipating, and hence controlling, the reader's reaction. At the other end of Ellison's novel, the response is different. The reader has read all that Invisible Man has tortured himself to chronicle, a life of mistakes and mistaken identities that is useless unless he "at least *tell*[s] a few people about it." Ellison's essays and fiction are dedicated to the creation of a more equitable society, one premised on civility, equal treatment under the law, and the cultivation of human dignity. Or, as he says in his essays, art and democracy should converge in their shared dedication "to the development of conscious, articulate citizens."

Invisible Man's paradigmatic life enlightens us regarding the fallout that occurs when society fails to institute these principles and falls short of what it has promised. In the end *Invisible Man is* a protest book, but is also unusually introspective. Invisible Man must recreate himself, before he can even think about reconstructing the world around him. "[T]he true darkness lies within my own mind," he says. With this single, vital and victorious insight he becomes conscious and conscientious of others, especially of the reader on whom he is dependent, a listener to his solitary voice in the darkness. What he offers in return, "Who knows that, on lower frequencies, I speak for you?" is a kinship not of skin color but of something deeper, lower, and more frequent—it is the intimacy of the shared breath of humanity.

JOHN M. REILLY

The Testament of Ralph Ellison

Suppose we take Ralph Ellison at his word when he tells us that the basic significance of the essays and occasional pieces collected in *Shadow and Act* is autobiographical.[1] Then, despite the omission from this version of a life writing of dates and particularized events that would mark it as an objective chronicle of the passage from youth to maturity and obscurity to fame, the reader's expectation that the autobiography will depict a destiny is met by Ellison's repeated mention of the essential experience that forms the condition for his life's project.

The dominant feature emerging from his reflective viewpoint is the good fortune he had being brought up in Oklahoma, whose settlement by black and white Americans hardly more than a generation before his birth exempted its society, for a time, from the equilibrium of rigid caste relationships prevalent in the Old South and the fixed systems of power characteristic of the capitalist industrial sectors of the United States. It was a newer America where he was born, and, though soon enough it fastened upon itself the rites of racial segregation and the forms of a class society, during the early years of its statehood and Ellison's life, Oklahoma recapitulated in the minds of its citizens, if not entirely in the circumstances of their material lives, the situation of the American frontier. Exhilarated by the sense of possibility in a loosely structured community, the young Ellison and his confrères could

From *Speaking for You: The Vision of Ralph Ellison*, ed. Kimberly W. Benston. © 1987 by John M. Reilly. Reprinted by permission.

imaginatively transcend the categories of race, thinking of themselves as
the "Renaissance men" of an American comedy rather than as victims in
a racist melodrama.

Through the selections of memory and the emphases of rhetoric,
Ellison invests the musicians who created the vernacular idiom of the
region's native music—Southwestern jazz—with the authority of
practical philosophers on his latter-day frontier. In the outlaw status
earned by their exclusion and willed separation from the company of
respectable judges, ministers, and politicians who were the agents of
repressive "civilization," the jazzmen embodied in the art for which
they lived the attributes of popular archetype. Their versatility and
improvisational style evinced the idealized individualism of American
legend and evoked the witty triumphs of Afro-American folk heroes,
while in the processions of their art they performed a kind of
democratic enactment, singing the self in musical phrases that
combined in an utterance *en masse*. True jazz, Ellison writes

> is an art of individual assertion within and against the group.
> Each true jazz moment ... springs from a contest in which
> each artist challenges all the rest; each solo flight, or
> improvisation, represents (like the successive canvases of a
> painter) a definition of his identity; as individual, as member
> of the collectivity and as a link in the chain of tradition.
> (*S&A*, 234)

The climax of Ellison's projection of the importance of the
frontier in his life is, of course, his own emergence as an artist.
Exuberance and ambition allied with incontestable talent impelled him,
as it did the jazzmen, to creative expression as a means of self-definition.
It diminishes his accomplishment not at all to say that this was a result
of personality more than of conviction that he possessed prodigious
abilities. Taking up writing, he says, depended upon the chance of
Richard Wright's asking him to do a review and then a short story for
New Challenge magazine. Even so, writing "was a reflex of reading, an
extension of a source of pleasure, escape and instruction" (*S&A*, xii).
And before that, the composition of music for which he originally
hoped to prepare himself appears to have signified less an immersion in
a process than the hope of achieving a state of being, as in *being* another

Richard Wagner by composing a great symphony before the age of twenty-six. Furthermore, there was a good deal of serendipity and scarcely any sense of determinism bringing him to New York and within the reach of Wright's literary suggestions before he completed the prescribed course of formal study at Tuskegee Institute. A problem about his scholarship and the lure of the city he knew from Alain Locke's *The New Negro* as the setting of a contemporary "Renaissance" led him to yet another frontier.

Ellison's mention in *Shadow and Act*, and elsewhere, of writers from whose friendship and example he learned something of craft—Eliot, Hemingway, Malraux, Wright—has unquestionable interest, but not because they constitute a list of influences to be discerned in his writing. Rather, these references complete the imaginative paradigm of the inceptive autobiography by introducing his companions in the free republic of letters, an environment whose inhabitants define themselves through works undertaken individually, as members of the collectivity, and as links in the chains of tradition. A life of literature can be a difficult, combative one, but it is lived, Ellison tells us, in a zone of undiscovered possibilities that is the natural home and destiny of a man formed and conditioned by the historical and cultural environment of America's last physical frontier.

Intriguing as the factual details Ellison provides us of his life may be, they are insufficient to satisfy fully our curiosity. In "The World and the Jug" (*S&A*, 141), he asks Irving Howe to remember that an act of Chekhov's "was significant only because Chekhov was *Chekhov*, the great writer." So, because Ralph Ellison is *Ralph Ellison*, we should like to know all manner of things about his life in the hope that they could "explain" him, and, if not that, at least give us the fullest possible description of the man. But *Shadow and Act* offers a truncated autobiography. Even with the addition of writings not collected in that volume, we have only the framework of a life, and a subjectively rendered framework, at that. Ellison has situated his life for us within a broadly outlined episode of history resonant of the schemes of Frederick Jackson Turner and the images of popular culture. It is a generalized, a priori picture that will not reveal how the unique Ralph Ellison, equipped with certain predispositions, actually became the particular man. "Negroness" is nothing like a metaphysical condition, he says.

It is not skin color which makes a Negro American but
cultural heritage as shaped by the American experience, the
social and political predicament, a sharing of that "concord
of sensibilities" which the group expresses through
historical circumstances.... (*S&A*, 131)

What, then, are the features of person, the experiences in family and
intimate relationships that particularized Ellison's assumption of the
Afro-American cultural heritage and, thus, individualizes him within
the group? He does not say.

It might be objected that this is a querulous response to the casual
remark Ellison makes about the autobiographical significance of *Shadow
and Act*. Perhaps. But to note that the plot of a life we glimpse only in
fragments dispersed throughout his essays is an abstract representation
of the self establishes two crucial points for understanding his
nonfiction. The first point is that Ellison presents himself as a symbolic
figure in whose portrayal the absence of particularized data encourages
us to see a typical product of the American frontier. Moreover, in
delineating his experience among a people who intentionally left the
realm of slavery to make a new way, he indicates that the frontier effects
the necessary rupture in the repetitive order of social oppression that
gives birth to history. Like the protagonist of *Invisible Man*, who claims
to speak for all of us on one frequency or another, Ellison the essayist
stands at the beginning of self-determining Afro-American history. The
second crucial point to observe about the generalized autobiography is
that its broad frontiersman scheme is obviously a fiction, not in the
sense that it bears no relationship to a reality that can be documented
from other sources, but rather it is like fiction in the selectivity it uses
to enforce the compelling significance of a single, unqualified feature of
Ellison's life: his certain and intuitive resolve to achieve the birthright
of a free citizen of a democracy.

So the apparent autobiography in *Shadow and Act* is an exemplum;
yet, in its purpose it is more than that. It provides the authenticating
image for a volume of writing devoted to exploration of classical issues
in American social philosophy. As it discusses democracy from the
unusual vantage point of an aesthetic concept of self-realization,
Ellison's fragmentary autobiography certifies that the source of
discussion is a representative Afro-American.

The Afro-American, as citizen and artist, engages in a continual struggle against reductive stereotype, not merely the Negrophobic characterizations of vicious racists, but also the interpretations of black life advanced by a social science that describes its object almost entirely by reference to the dominant white majority. Nineteenth-century students of the "Negro problem" applied their supposed science to demonstration of the black's comparative inferiority, thereby creating a justification for continued exploitation. More "progressive" thought in the twentieth century has redefined the condition once perceived as subhuman as a situation wherein blacks are the victims of whites. In either interpretation Afro-Americans are conceived as existing in dependency. Even the corrective work of Gunnar Myrdal, whose influential study *An American Dilemma* earns Ellison's praise for discrediting the "non-scientific nonsense that has cluttered our sociological literature" (*S&A*, 305), must be eventually disqualified as a truthful or useful tool for understanding, because despite its microscopic empirical analyses it retains in conclusion the reductive idea that "the Negro's entire life and, consequently, also his opinions on the Negro problem are, in the main, to be considered as secondary reactions to more primary pressures from the side of the dominant white majority" (*S&A*, 315). Ellison's displeasure with this conclusion would seem to be phrased moderately enough to suit the decorum of an academic journal, but in 1944, when the review failed to be published in the *Antioch Review*, maybe it was a different story. Nevertheless, it took twenty years before Ellison could explain the point of difference between that famous study of the Negro and the perspective of the critic whose source of knowledge is the living of a Negro life. "Can a people," Ellison asks,

> live and develop for over three hundred years simply by *reacting*? Are American Negroes simply the creation of white men, or have they at least helped to create themselves out of what they found around them? Men have made a way of life in caves and upon cliffs, why cannot Negroes have made a life upon the horns of the white man's dilemma? (*S&A*, 316)

Ellison could easily be bringing ethical proof to his commentary on Myrdal and the traditions of American social science. Common sense dictates that he ought to be qualified by "Negroness" to evaluate discussions of Afro-American social reality. The common-sense assumption will not pertain, however, in the face of the closed systems erected on the premises of stereotypes. These systems hold that opinions of Negroes are products of dependency, too, and Ellison has no inclination to counter with an invocation of racial mysticism. The counterattack would be as irrational as the view it meant to rebut is absurd. In any case, the contest with stereotypes is not a simple matter of posing truth, even the truth of personal testimony, against falsity. The "struggle over the nature of reality" (*S&A*, 26) does not concern data. Nor does it involve contrary perceptions. What the struggle is about is conceptions, the patterns and forms men and women construct from their observations and by their actions to give life a shape.

The function of stereotypes is instrumental. Arising "from an internal psychological state ... from an inner need to believe" (*S&A*, 28), bigotry seizes upon the stock ideas current in social exchange to sanction irrational needs with the plausible appearance of overgeneralized evidence. To complicate the matter, other intellectual structures spring from personal needs by a similar process. Ellison's explicit example is art, which psychologically

> represents the socialization of some profoundly personal problem involving guilt (often symbolic murder—parricide, fratricide—incest, homosexuality, all problems at the base of personality) from which by expressing them along with other elements (images, memories, emotions, ideas) he [the artist] seeks transcendence. To be effective as personal fulfillment, if it is to be more than dream, the work of art must simultaneously evoke images of reality and give them formal organization. And it must, since the individual's emotions are formed in society, shape them into socially meaningful patterns. (*S&A*, 39)

Somewhere between the pathology of bigotry and the sublimation of profound art occurs the use of stereotype that amounts to a linguistic redundancy, the repetition of customary formulas without examination of their implications. The continuum of conceptions interests Ellison much less for its genesis hidden in the fog of singular psyches than for its significance in fostering or obstructing the progress of democracy. The instrumentality of concepts working in relation to democracy he images as a dialectic of texts.

During his literary apprenticeship among left-wing American writers, Ralph Ellison was familiar with the plan of the Communist party of the United States to establish a black republic in the South ("Study," 421). Although the plan has been criticized by anti-Communists as an alien notion, it attracted the interest of Richard Wright and other blacks who viewed it as a synthesis of nationalism and socialism. The program for the autonomous republic was built upon an analysis of the lower South, where blacks had been historically a majority in certain contiguous counties, had shared a common life in agricultural production, and had evolved distinctive institutions;[2] thus, the Black Belt, by this analysis, met Stalin's definition of a nation as "a historically evolved, stable community of language, territory, economic life and psychological make-up manifested in a community of culture."[3] Apart from the political campaign in which it was used, Stalin's description of a nation is hardly remarkable. It is in fact consistent with a current of American thought beginning in Crevecoeur's *Letters from an American Farmer* and continuing to the present to define American character by association with a unique social and physical environment. Yet the truly remarkable thing is that Ellison offers his conception of the origin of the American nation without regard to material and social history or to a current in American writing with which in other contexts he shows unquestionable sympathy:

> We began as a nation not through the accidents of race or religion or geography ... but when a group of men, some of them political philosophers, put down, upon what we now recognize as quite sacred papers, their conception of the nation which they intended to establish on these shores. They described, as we know, the obligations of the state to the citizen, of the citizen to the state; they committed themselves to certain ideas of justice, just as they committed us to a system which would guarantee all of its citizens equality of opportunity. (*S&A*, 163–64)

Again, when he speaks in a later essay, "The Little Man at Chehaw Station," of the struggle to define the corporate American identity, he establishes the site of conflict as intellectual:

> The terrain upon which we struggle is itself abstract, a terrain of ideas that, although man-made, exert the compelling force of the ideal, of the sublime; ideas that draw their power from the Declaration of Independence, the Constitution, and the Bill of Rights. We stand, as we say, united in the name of these sacred principles. But, indeed, it is in the name of these same principles that we ceaselessly contend, affirming our ideals even as we do them violence. ("Little Man," 34)

According to these definitions, America, and especially the American character, are voluntarist creations, the dialectic of their development abstracted from the circumstances of material processes to the level of the word.

In its search for an essence, Ellison's image of etiology endows America with the characteristics of intentional documents. Assuming the aura of philosophical principles, the history of America, which is to say a history of texts, is all consequential to their appearance. For documents of universal significance there can be no point to an inquiry into the recesses of the authors' psychology or even the particular circumstances that made up their original context. Instead, what is pertinent is a history from the point of view of efforts to realize, or evade, the meaning of those sacred documents, a history that is a record of intended effects and that is apprehensible through the symbolic actions and cross references of succeeding texts. Such a history becomes the primary theme of Ralph Ellison's nonfiction.

Among the most important works succeeding upon the axiomatic democratic documents are novels, instances of a literary genre that in America has always been tied up with the idea of nationhood, because it is "a form which deals with change in human personality and human society," that is, with individual and social life that has broken the cake of custom. In treating its inevitable subject the American novel brings "to the surface those values, those patterns of conduct, those dilemmas, psychological and technological, which abide within the human predicament," thereby proposing answers to the questions: What are we? Who are we? ("Novel," 1023). The tentative and open form of the novel associates with democratic philosophy; its morality confirms an identity between democracy and fiction. "The novel," Ellison explains in an interview, "is a complex agency for the symbolic depiction of experience, and it demands that the writer be willing to look at both sides of characters and issues.... You might say that the form of the novel imposes its morality upon the novelist by demanding a complexity of vision and an openness to the variety and depth of experience" ("Study," 428).

Ellison sees the discussion of the nature of democratic life taking place in texts, but this is not to say he believes reality is exclusively linguistic, or that the texts embodying the varied concepts of democratic life exist autonomously. Using his exemplary autobiography to illustrate the origins of an outlook, he offers an ample listing in "Hidden Name and Complex Fate" of the materials he gathered for art in his formative years. In addition to weather, the sounds of black people's voices, and experiences of the physical world reminiscent of the catalogued responses of Richard Wright's sensibility that impressed him when he reviewed *Black Boy* (*S&A*, 81), Ellison cites the characters of players of the "dozens," fortunetellers, bootleggers, "men who did anything well," blind blues singers, "Negroes who were part Indian ... and Indians who had children who lived in towns as Negroes, ... certain Jews, Mexicans, Chinese cooks, a German orchestra conductor and an English grocer who owned a Franklin touring car. And certain Negro mechanics ... who had so assimilated the automobile that they seemed to be behind a steering wheel even as they walked the streets or danced with girls. And there were the whites who despised us and the others who shared our hardships and our joys" (*S&A*, 158–59). Each figure independently suggests an anecdote that might develop as a story of uniqueness; collectively they defy the expectations of categorization by race, class, or type. Like the legendary jazzmen they imply a transcendence of the limits upon the self. Their lives, too, might be art, and, in telling of their diversity, the writer like Ellison would appropriate from life the sense of human potentiality and plasticity that links the values of fiction with the principles of democracy.

"The novel," Ellison declares, "is a way of possessing life, of slowing it down, and giving it the writer's own sense of values in a deliberately and subtly structured way" ("Novel," 1023), which is another way of saying that art objectifies the subjective experiences, making available to the audience the substance of a consciousness that through the discipline of art—its morality and techniques—has acquired a way of seeing and feeling, summoning and directing the imagination (*S&A*, 162).

Ellison's faith in the novel depends upon a further point that is implicit in his adoption of a speaking voice in some of his writings, his evident interest in readings of the classic American novels, and the metaphor for audience he presents as the little man at Chehaw Station. Fiction is social communication. It exists only as it is read. The reader's subjectivity is equally important as the writer's consciousness objectified in the text. The novel is a product of the self and, at the same time, becomes something different from the self, namely, an object in the world. The reader who discerns and participates in the writer's intention by recovering the transmuted world in art freely chooses to enter a contract with the writer by the terms of which art becomes a collective enterprise. Thus, writer and reader form a community of free equals offering by their relationship a prevision of a fuller democracy. In the works of Mark Twain, Herman Melville, Stephen Crane, *and* Ralph Ellison, the prevision gains added sanction from the direct attention given to democracy by writers with an abiding faith in it, but even writers who ignore democratic obligations altogether participate in the community of freedom that distinguishes the aesthetic dimension of life. They can not choose to do otherwise. Nothing could be more important, then, than creating structures of reality that are consistent with their artistic medium, and no recognition could be more significant to the artist than that he or she engages in the democratic culture.

Ellison's dislike of hard-boiled individualistic writers grows out of a belief that their techniques and outlook contradict the quality of aesthetic community, but criticism of hard-boiled mannerism is comparatively easy. Much more difficult is developing a criterion to distinguish the stereotype on a philosophical level from the profound structures of democratically enhancing art that arise, we recall, in similarly subjective ways. Complexity of reference is one measure but not a sufficient one, because Ellison's own concepts often display a simplified eloquence echoing the "self-evident" declarations of eighteenth-century political writing. The inadequacy of stereotypes, starkly asserted or embedded in complex writing, is to be discerned in their employment of false resolutions to the basic contradictions of American experience.

America's "founders asserted the noble idea of creating a free, open society while retaining slavery, a system in direct contradiction to their rhetorically inclusive concept of freedom. Thus, from the beginning, racism has mocked the futuristic dream of democracy" ("Essential," 137). Stereotypes confront this contradiction with "symbolic magic" by which "the white American seeks to resolve the dilemma arising between his democratic beliefs and certain antidemocratic practices, between his acceptance of the sacred democratic belief that all men are created equal and his treatment of every tenth man as though he were not" (S&A, 28). Patently ridiculous representations of blacks as biologically unfit to participate in democratic fraternity resolve the contradiction between practice and belief with racist myth. Yet, even among those made queasy by overt racism, a racial segregation persists within the mind, as though the reconciliation of North and South that provided the dénouement to the Civil War and Reconstruction by effectively excluding blacks from the national economic and political life also erased them from white public memory.

According to Ellison's reading, the black once served as the inevitable symbol of humanity in literature written by the generation that spanned the time of the Civil War, and the rebelliousness of authors repulsed by the conventional evil of "civilization" projected fraternal association of blacks and whites as their social ideal (S&A, 32–33). Alas, by the mid-twentieth century it was no longer true. The Negro remained resident in the American consciousness to the extent that "it is practically impossible for the white Americans to think of sex, of economics, his children or womenfolk, or of sweeping socio-political changes, without summoning ... fear-flecked images of black men." But now the white American, even the literary artist, rejects his own consciousness "discarding an ambiguous substance which the artists of other cultures would confront boldly and humanize into the stuff of tragic art" (S&A, 100). Legalized racism of the past was an outrageous denial of human community, but the evasion of the significance of the black in contemporary public discourse is equally outrageous, for it is an act of bad faith, positing a separation of white and black that cannot, and did not, in fact, ever exist. Failing to confront the existence of black Americans even for the purpose of constructing a myth to resolve the contradiction between pragmatic morality and the creed that supposedly informs our institutional life, the new segregationists of the intellect invalidate their own conceptions of reality and can produce only more stereotypes.

Finally, in addition to exposing the stereotypes of racists and the segregationists of the intellect, there is the more subtle problem of judging and describing the inadequacy of the social science Ellison deplores. This sort of writing on the Afro-American does not conspicuously evade the contradiction between professions of Americanism and its practices; still, as his review of Myrdal and his response to Irving Howe indicate, Ellison sees in the sociological habit of thought no chance of texts that will be worthy of the democratic literary tradition. Melville or Twain could emplot their fictions as tragedy because of their conceptions of the black in society, but no tragedy can pertain when the actors are defined as objects of history disabled by their exterior circumstances from imitating the legendary figures of the Oklahoma frontier and leaping the boundaries of the enclosing circle that enforcers of practical order think they can draw about the alien blacks. Ellison is probably convinced that most of the new "friends of the Negro" mean well, but in their own way, he might say, the concepts embodying and expressing their concern for blacks are still little better than segregationist, because they do not acknowledge human kinship beneath outward circumstances.

Those who struggle over the definition of American reality are united in a dialectic that replicates the reciprocal relationships that characterize America. Particularly on the level of culture there is an irrepressible movement toward integration illustrated, among other ways, by the three examples of cultural pluralism in "The Little Man at Chehaw Station": (1) a recollection of the Tuskegee teacher who taught Ellison never to substitute mere technique for artful structure of emotion—that teacher, Hazel Harrison, had been a successful concert performer, a student of Ferruccio Busoni, and a friend of world-renowned figures in music, including Sergei Prokofiev, who presented her with a signed manuscript; (2) his observations of "a light-skinned, blue-eyed, Afro-American-featured young man" clad in dashiki and

English riding clothes who set up a reflex camera on Riverside Drive to photograph himself in histrionic poses beside a customized Volkswagen Beetle; and (3) his anecdote of a startling encounter in a basement of the formerly black section of New York City called San Juan Hill, with coal heavers who carried on an expert discussion of operatic technique they had learned by years of appearances as extras at the Metropolitan Opera in the southern idiomatic vernacular of formally uneducated Afro-American workingmen. The latter occurrence especially seemed a great "American joke ... centered on the incongruities of race, economic status, and culture" that vastly extended his "appreciation of the arcane ways of American cultural possibility" ("Little Man," 48).

Any comprehensive study of American music, dance, language, costume, cuisine, or, for that matter, mating practices might provide the evidence to substantiate Ellison's impressionistic anecdotes and put the lie to the notion that the races are separate. Useful as such proof of syncretism might be as further illustration of democratic exchange, Ellison's main interest in culture remains disclosure of the motive for creation. "Who wills to be a Negro?" he asks at one point in *Shadow and Act*. "*I* do!" (*S&A*, 132). And so do the musicians who play black music and the storytellers whose tales project their Afro-American identity in an improvised vernacular that is the equivalent of jazz. Again and again he proclaims that cultural expression comes from the urge to control reality. The blues, he says in explanation, is "an assertion of the irrepressibly human over all circumstances whether created by others or by one's own human failings" (*S&A*, 246). The voice of his long-time friend Jimmy Rushing carries a "rock-bottom sense of reality, coupled with our sense of the possibility of rising above it" (*S&A*, 242). And although the blues is not obvious political protest, it is "an art form and thus a transcendence of those conditions created within the Negro community by the denial of social justice" (*S&A*, 257). No wonder Jimmy Rushing, Charlie Christian, and Mahalia Jackson appear in the essays as leaders of ritual in the community. Their performance draws the audience into a sacred rite celebrating the musician-hero and affirming the presence within their ceremony of the central principle of collective Afro-American life—the control of destiny by aesthetic will that was once the slaves' means of humanizing their servitude.

Ellison has been criticized for weighing the material circumstances of oppression too lightly in the balance with his convictions about this power of Afro-American cultural initiative. Apart from his sympathetic exposition of Richard Wright's "almost unrelieved picture of a personality corrupted by brutal environment" (*S&A*, 81), Ellison writes only twice at length about the bleakness of oppression. Once is the essay "The Way It Is," originally printed in *New Masses*. In this reconstructed interview, a Harlem woman voices the bitterness she feels about sacrificing for the war effort of a country that evidently intends to do nothing about "all the little Hitlers over here" (*S&A*, 289). This is the closest Ellison may have ever come to the familiar mode of protest writing. Just as unique in the Ellison canon is the piece titled "Harlem is Nowhere," unprinted before *Shadow and Act*. In a discussion of the Lafargue Clinic's psychiatric treatment of patients without defense against the chaos that threatens their personalities, he comes nearer than anywhere else to attempting a total analysis of the Afro-American condition. The report mentions that "talented youths ... leap through the development of decades in a brief twenty years" (*S&A*, 296), but its burden is description of the people who stumble through anxiety and alienation because their abrupt arrival in the modern world has stripped them of the supports of traditional folk culture, while for the old reasons of racial discrimination they are denied a place in a new institutional life that might nurture them through change. In a rare combination of the approach of historical anthropology and the philosophy of democratic idealism, Ellison limns *this* Harlem as an area of perverse freedom, the home base, perhaps, of Bliss Proteus Rinehart.

These exceptional departures of Ellison's from his usual stance in nonfiction point up the genuine need for a defense of his work against the charge that it takes too sanguine a view of Afro-American life, because it ordinarily minimizes the effects of material reality. For all his concern with combating the vicious and dehumanizing stereotypes, his struggle over the nature of reality takes place on the level of concept; and despite the undoubted attraction of the frontiersman's autobiography and the celebratory characterizations of black artists, these portrayals may be said to be just momentary pauses between the beats of day-to-day living.

There is no possibility of converting the criticism into a depiction of Ellison as an ingenuous optimist. On the contrary, he has no doubt that evil will always define the plot of the American story and some form of victimization will always be with us, although he aims to see that racial prejudice will not determine the designation of evil or scapegoat (*Interviews*, 69–70). Whether we call that conservatism or realism, Ellison's nonfiction still must be seen as conducting its campaign on a site that even by analogy cannot be identified with the location of the socioeconomic conflict that necessarily preoccupies the mass of black people.

Nevertheless there is a ready defense to be made, and it is not sophistically tricky, equivocal, or dependent upon establishing culture as a superior reality. Ralph Ellison is not evasive or casuistic. In a paraphrase of Kenneth Burke, his favorite theorist, he says that the words evoking democratic principles are

> charismatic terms for transcendent order.... Being forms of symbolic action, they tend, through their nature as language, to sweep us in tow as they move by a process of linguistic negation toward the ideal. As a form of symbolic action, they operate by negating nature as a given and amoral condition, creating endless series of man-made or man-imagined positives.... In this way ... man uses language to moralize both nature and himself. ("Little Man," 35)

So, of course, these words are involved in a search for a system of aesthetics and they influence our expositions in the area of artistic form, but precisely how do they actually become active influences in the realm of sociopolitical life? Here the argument needs a development that must be inferred from the tone and total effect of Ellison's nonfiction.

The subsystem of language in art is social as well as symbolic action, social for the reasons explained in the discussion of the community of writer and reader as a prevision of democracy, active because the qualitative difference of aesthetic language from the immediate physical world generates new behavior. Detaching themselves from the empirical world in order to apprehend the recreated world of art, writers, performers, and their audiences experience reality with its shape and underlying principles laid open by virtue of art's conceptual structures. The world in art presents a more complete entity than the empirical world; thus, it becomes an engaging totality without mystification, yet at the same time a totality possessing the power to enhance life through appropriation of the significance of reality to consciousness. The processes of art, its creation and reception, found a zone of freedom, even for the oppressed. The audience recognizes human intention, a piece of deliberate work, in the creation of the aesthetic artifact. Collaborating in the task of completing the work or artifact, the reader or listener finds immanent his or her own freedom and possibility of intentional action. Moreover, the substance of art induces reflection, perhaps through recognition of plausibility in the story, admiration of technique, or identification with a character to accompany identification with the artist. That reflection experienced as discovery redresses the sense of powerlessness and alienation previously felt amid the welter of routine events. Set free, however briefly, by the aid of art, the audience is prepared to abandon spontaneous or reflexive behavior and to act with the same deliberate intention as the artists toward the world. For example, in the communion of the blues the audience joins with the singer to supplant suffering with the splendid control of tragicomic lyricism, or readers of *Invisible Man* who join the protagonist in his quest realize that because their own identity, like his, entails no obligation to the expectations of others, they have achieved a decisive moment of self-knowledge and are free to make themselves in action.

Shadow and Act has much further use, too, as a guide to Ellison's fiction. As he points out in his *Paris Review* interview, each section of *Invisible Man* "begins with a sheet of paper; each piece of paper is exchanged for another and contains a definition of his identity, or the social role he is to play as defined by others" (S&A, 177). In other words, a contest of concepts regarding American reality conducted through textual relations and interrelations forms an armature for the novel's plot, and not only in the representation of literal texts, but also through the associations of simulated speeches and metaphoric descriptions that read as texts of commentary about approximations and departures from the intent of the principal documents that founded the ideal of American democracy. Together this intertextuality within the complex enveloping form of the novel constitutes Ellison's assessment of the contradictions in which the possibility of making history is born.

The making of history—Ellison's ultimate subject—has subjective significance, for the freedom to act intentionally and humanize the world arises in consciousness. One becomes an historical actor by coming to know one can transcend the conditions made by others. The anecdotes and selective memories we receive as Ellison's inchoate autobiography in the nonfiction take their tone and form from the need to represent the first emergence of what philosophers would call his project. We feel the episodes are fragmentary, because doubtless the sense of the possibility of becoming one's own product could only have been seen in glimpses, at first. Acquaintance with purposive life awaited his meeting with musicians in the black community whose witness he celebrates in the essays grouped under the rubric "Sound and Mainstream." The discipline enabling Ellison to initiate his own transcendent project he discovered through literature, the art whose semantic and referential nature can synthesize the entire range of human experience. Finally, through the happy accident of living in the culture of a nation preoccupied with its social novelty, Ellison located in the founding texts of America the words that addressed his emergence as a writer as well as a citizen. Thus, the subtext of *Shadow and Act* charts the evolution of its author's conscious motive. Here are the particulars that will be overlooked if the reader looks for a conventionally drawn autobiography, particulars that explain the necessity to counter stereotypes that would deny his capacity, because of his race, to enter history as a conscious player. As a self-determining figure, then, he writes his primary text—the evidently topical discussions—out of devotion to confronting the American contradiction of race and democracy with a theory meant to surpass the contradiction, a theory explaining the appearance of a synthetic democratic culture that acquires its requisite vigor from the Afro-American arts.

Let us, therefore, take Ralph Ellison at his word when he tells us that the significance of *Shadow and Act* is basically autobiographical, not because he tells us things that can interest us only because he is a famous writer, but because this autobiographer addresses the fundamental literary question: Why write? In the answer he gives, we find both the essential Ralph Ellison and his compelling democratic testament.

NOTES

1. Ralph Ellison, in the Introduction to *Shadow and Act*, xviii. All subsequent citations of this source appear in text as *S&A*.

2. The position was developed most fully in James S. Allen, *The Negro Question in America*.

3. Joseph Stalin, *Marxism and the National and Colonial Question* (London: n.d.), 8. [A paperback edition of this work was printed in the U.S.]

WORKS CITED

Allen, James S. *The Negro Question in America*. New York: International, 1936.

Ellison, Ralph. "The Essential Ellison." Interview by Ishmael Reed, Quincy Troupe, Steve Cannon. *Y'Bird Reader* 1 (Autumn 1977): 126–59.

———. "The Little Man at Chehaw Station: The American Artist and His Audience." *American Scholar* 47 (Winter 1977–78): 25–48.

———. "The Novel as a Function of American Democracy." *Wilson Library Bulletin* (June 1967): 1022–27.

———. *Shadow and Act*. New York: Random House, 1964.

———. "Study and Experience: An Interview with Ralph Ellison." With Michael S. Harper and Robert B. Stepto. *Massachusetts Review* 18 (Autumn 1977): 417–435.

O'Brien, John, ed. *Interviews with Ten Black Writers*. New York: Liveright, 1973.

Stalin, Joseph. *Marxism and the National and Colonial Question*. London: n.d. Also: San Francisco: Proletarian Pubs., 1975.

C. W. E. BIGSBY

Improvising America: Ralph Ellison and the Paradox of Form

Writing in 1937, Richard Wright insisted that "black writers are being called upon to do no less than create values by which the race is to struggle, live and die."[1] In 1941 Ellison echoed this sentiment. His responsibility, he felt, was "to create the consciousness of his oppressed nation."[2] It was a stance he was later to be accused of abandoning by those who, in the 1960s and 1970s, proposed their own prescriptions for cultural and political responsibility and who found his determined pluralism unacceptable. For although he undeniably concentrated on the black experience in America, he tended to see this experience in relation to the problem of identity, the anxieties associated with the struggle for cultural autonomy, and the need to define the contours of experience. His central concern was with the relationship between raw experience and the shaping power of the imagination. And, for him, the "imagination itself is *integrative*," in that it is essentially involved in the process of "making symbolic wholes out of parts."[3] Such a stance plainly has implications on a moral and social level no less than on an artistic one.

He has, indeed, always been fascinated, politically, ethically, and aesthetically, with the struggle to discover form in diversity. To his mind this was equally the problem of the Negro in America, of the individual in a democracy, and of the artist confronted with the sheer contingency

From *Speaking for You: The Vision of Ralph Ellison.* © 1987 by C.W.E. Bigsby. Reprinted by permission.

and flux of events. The imaginative linking of these experiences, indeed the metaphoric yoking of the processes of invention in life and art, is a characteristic of Ellison's artistic strategy and of his moral assumptions. But it is a process which, from the beginning, he acknowledged to be fraught with ambiguity, for he was not unaware that form could imply entrapment as well as release. Thus, he argued that "for the novelist, of any cultural or racial identity, his form is his greatest freedom and his insights are where he finds them," while acknowledging that that form potentially defines the limits of his freedom.[4] To use story or myth to control experience is also, potentially, to imprison oneself in the prison house of myth. Archetype too easily becomes stereotype. To deploy language as a means of inducing coherencies is to subordinate oneself to the constraints of that language, which is, at the very least, historically stained. Thus for the writer, as for the American pioneer, "the English language and traditional cultural forms served both as guides and as restraints, anchoring Americans in the wisdom and processes of the past, while making it difficult for them to perceive with any clarity the nuances of their new identity" (*MR* 431). It is a paradox that lies at the heart of all of his work. For Ellison, the act of writing is an act of shaping inchoate experience into moral meaning no less than aesthetic form. But it is an act that implies its own coercions. It implicates the imagination in the process of control.

This tension between chaos and form, this recognition of a profound ambivalence, is a fundamental trope of Ellison's work. He seems captivated by paradox, fascinated by apparent contradictions, drawn to the polarities of American experience, simultaneously attracted and repelled by the nervous energy of the unformed and the compelling grace of coalescence. Even his prose style seems often to turn around sets of dualities that are fused together by the writer, contained by the imagination, and exemplified in the linguistic structure, as he believes they can be so fused in the world beyond the page.

Thus, while he readily identified the metonymic reductivism implied in white attempts to mythologize Negro life, insisting that "the Negro stereotype is really an image of the unorganized, irrational forces of American life, forces through which, by projecting them in forms of images of an easily dominated minority, the white individual seeks to be at home in the vast unknown world of America," he nonetheless asserted that without myths, "chaos descends, faith vanishes and superstitions prowl in the mind" (S&A, 41). The same process contains a generative and a destructive potential.

So, too, with language. We are, Ellison insists, "language using, language misusing animals—beings who are by nature vulnerable to both the negative *and* the positive promptings of language as symbolic action."[5] He addresses this ambivalence directly in an essay called, "Twentieth-Century Fiction and the Black Mask of Humanity," where he suggests, "Perhaps the most insidious and least understood form of segregation is that of the word. And by this I mean the word in all its complex formulations, from the proverb to the novel and stage play, the word with all its subtle power to suggest and foreshadow overt action while magically disguising the moral consequences of that action and providing it with symbolic and psychological justification. For if the word has the potency to revive and make us free, it also has the power to blind, imprison and destroy." Indeed, to him "the essence of the word is its ambivalence" (S&A, 24–25), more especially in a society in which the nature of the real is problematic for reasons of racial ideology. This suspicion marks all of his work, from the nonfunctional articulateness of his protagonist in the early short story "Flying Home," through the deceptive speeches and documents of *Invisible Man*, to the uncontrolled rhetoric of the narrator of his later short story, "A Song of Innocence," who observes, "They say that folks misuse words but I see it the other way around, words misuse people. Usually when you think you're saying what you mean you're really saying what the words want you to say.... Words are tricky.... No matter what you try to do, words can never mean meaning."[6]

Melville had made much the same point and addressed the same ambivalence with respect to the urge to subordinate chaos to form. He, too, was aware that language itself constitutes the primary mechanism of the shaping imagination and it was not for nothing that Ellison chose to quote from *Benito Cereno* as an epigraph to his own novel. For Captain Delano, in that story, uses language as an agent of power and control, albeit a language rendered ironic by his moral and intellectual blindness; while Benito Cereno, imprisoned by a cunning and dominant black crew, who for the most part remain potently silent, deploys a language which is willfully opaque, hinting at truths that language cannot be entrusted to reveal. And yet language is the only medium through which the novelist can attempt to communicate his own truths. It was a familiar conundrum of nineteenth-century American writing and one to which Ellison was compulsively drawn.

The strict discipline and carefully sustained order of Delano's ship is an expression of his fear of an anarchy that he dare not imagine and cannot confront. And the image of that anarchy, for Delano and Cereno alike, is the Negro, whose shadow they see as falling across American history. But Melville suggests that just as their own ordered world contains its virus of moral anarchy, so what Delano takes for anarchy is perhaps a coherence he is afraid to acknowledge; the hieroglyphs of action that he chooses to translate as pure chaos can be decoded in a wholly different way. Indeed, Melville's story turns precisely on this ambiguity. So does much of Ellison's work.

Chaos and order constitute the twin poles of experience, promising, simultaneously, vital energy and destructive flux, necessary form but threatening stasis. Indeed, he is quite capable, in a single paragraph, of presenting both order and chaos as promise and threat. Speaking of the process whereby national identity coalesces from its constituent elements, he asserted, in 1953, "Our task then is always to challenge the apparent forms of reality—that is, the fixed manners and values of the few, and to struggle with it until it reveals its insights, its truth.... We are fortunate as American writers in that with our variety of racial and national traditions, idioms and manners we are yet one. On its profoundest level, American experience is of a whole. Its truth lies in its diversity and swiftness of change" (S&A, 106). The task for the writer would seem to be to inhabit these ambiguities and thereby to cast light not merely on processes endemic to art but also on the struggle that the individual and the race wage with contingency. Irresistibly drawn to the primal energy of flux, the writer, nonetheless, is inevitably committed to the creation of coherent form, thereby offering himself as a paradigm of the processes of self-invention and the distillation of cultural identity.

It is a theme that echoes throughout Ellison's work. Thus, he quotes approvingly André Malraux's observation that "the organized significance of art ... is stronger than all the multiplicity of the world ... that significance alone enables many to conquer chaos and to master destiny" (S&A, 83), while in an introduction to Stephen Crane's *Red Badge of Courage* he chose to stress "the shaping grace of Crane's imagination," whereby "the actual event is reduced to significant form ... each wave and gust of wind, each intonation of voice and gesture of limb combining to a single effect of meaning ... the raging sea of life" (S&A, 86) thereby being contained by an act of imaginative economy. He even insists that "in the very act of trying to create something there is implicit a protest against the way things are—a protest against man's vulnerability before the larger forces of society and the universe ... a protest against that which is, against the raw and unformed way that we come into the world ... to provide some sense of transcendence over the given."[7] And yet he equally acknowledges that it is precisely the fear of anarchy that leads to the creation of coercive models that express nothing more than a fear of the uncontrolled and the unknown. Thus, when Leslie Fiedler identifies a homoeroticism in the relationship between Twain's Huck Finn and the Negro slave Jim, he is, according to Ellison, in reality simply shouting out "his most terrifying name for chaos. Other things being equal he might have called it 'rape,' 'incest,' 'patricide' or 'miscegenation'" (S&A, 51). Order has no preemptive rights. It requires a moral as well as an aesthetic elegance.

The history of Ellison's creative life, from his early days as a putative musician throughout his career as a novelist and essayist, has in effect been concerned with exploring this paradox and identifying a way, at least on a metaphoric level, in which it could be resolved. To some degree he found it in music. He began his career as a would-be composer, and music has always provided a central source of imagery for him. Thus, in describing the reaction of the reader of fiction, he suggests that "his sensibilities are made responsive to artistic structuring of symbolic form" through "the rhetorical 'stops'" of his own "pieties—filial, sacred, racial" (AS, 30). The writer, meanwhile, is described as playing upon these sensibilities "as a pianist upon a piano" (AS, 31). But, what is more significant, he found in jazz and the blues a powerful image of the struggle to imprint meaning on experience, to reconcile the apparently contradictory demands of order and freedom. Like Richard Wright, he saw the blues as an attempt to "possess the meaning of his life" (S&A, 7), while jazz offered a model for the act of improvisation that lies at the heart of personal experience. Indeed the key word becomes "improvisation," which is made to stand for the act of self-invention that is the essence of a private and a public drive for meaning and identity. It is an integrative metaphor that links his sense of racial distinctiveness to what is essentially a pluralist position: "The delicate balance struck between strong individual personality and the group during those early jam sessions was a marvel of social organization. I had learned too that the end of all this discipline and technical mastery was the desire to express an affirmative way of life through its musical tradition and that this tradition insisted that each artist achieve his creativity within its frame ... and when they expressed their attitude toward the world it was with a fluid style that reduced the chaos of living to form" (S&A, 189–90).

Thus, it is characteristic that in his account of growing up in the Southwest he chose to stress what he calls "the chaos of Oklahoma," as he elsewhere spoke of "the chaos of American society" (C, 57), but set this against his own growing fascination with the ordered world of music and literature. It is characteristic, too, that through an extension of this logic he should identify that same tension first with the nature of the American frontier experience (still recent history for the Oklahoma of his birth), then with the jazz which emerged from that same region, and then with the nature of artistic creativity itself. The move is one from the real to the metaphoric, from the pure tone to its significant resonances. Thus, he insists, "ours was a chaotic community, still characterized by frontier attitudes and by that strange mixture of the naive and sophisticated, the benign and the malignant, which makes the past and present so confusing" (C, 57), only to go on to suggest that it is possible to "hear the effects of this in the Southwestern jazz of the 30s, that joint creation of artistically free and exuberantly creative adventurers, of artists who had stumbled upon the freedom lying within the restrictions of their musical tradition as within the limitations of their social background, and who in their own unconscious way set an example for any Americans, Negro or white, who would find themselves in the arts."[8]

And this was a key to Ellison's attempts to square the circle, to resolve the paradox. The problem for the jazz musician, as for any artist, was how to celebrate versatility and possibility in a form that seemingly denied both. The key is seen by Ellison as lying precisely in improvisation, the exercise of a personal freedom within the framework of the group, an act of invention that builds on but is not limited by inherited forms. This becomes both his metaphor for the process of artistic invention and the means whereby individual and group identity coalesce. In terms of writing this tended to be translated into an instinctive existentialism, at the level of theme, a picaresque narrative drive, and a prose style that could prove as fluid and flexible, and yet as controlled and subject to the harmonies of character and story, as the jazz musician is free and yet responsive to the necessities of rhythm and mood. In terms of social process it became a description of the means whereby diverse elements are harmonized. Thus, speaking of the origins of American national identity, Ellison remarked, "Out of the democratic principles set down on paper in the Constitution and the Bill of Rights they were improvising themselves into a nation, scraping together a conscious culture out of the various dialects, idioms, lingos, and mythologies of America's diverse peoples and regions." Similarly, in describing the relationship between black and white cultural forms, he observed that "the slaves ... having no past in the art of Europe ... could use its elements and their inherited sense of style to improvise forms through which they could express their own unique sense of African experience ... and white artists often found the slaves' improvisations a clue to their own improvisations" (*MR*, 431).

As a boy he had been taught the rudiments of orchestration, the blending, the integration, of different instruments to form an harmonic whole. It was offered to him as a lesson in the deconstruction of a score which was to enable him to "attack those things I desired so that I could pierce the mystery and possess them"; but in retrospect it becomes a lesson in civics. True jazz, he insists, "is an act of individual assertion within and against the group. Each true jazz moment ... springs from a contest in which each artist challenges all the rest; each solo flight, or improvisation, represents ... a definition of his identity: as individual, as member of the collectivity and as a link in the chain of tradition. Thus, because jazz finds its very life in an endless improvisation upon traditional materials, the jazzman must lose his identity even as he finds it" (*S&A*, 234). And, beyond this, jazz becomes an image of America itself, "fecund in its inventiveness, swift and traumatic in its resources" (*S&A*, 233).

The parallel between jazz and his own social circumstances, growing up in postfrontier Oklahoma, seems clear to Ellison in retrospect. "It is an important circumstance for me as a writer to remember," he wrote in 1964, "because while these musicians and their fellows were busy creating out of tradition, imagination, and the sounds and emotions around them, a freer, more complex, and driving form of jazz, my friends and I were exploring an idea of human versatility and possibility which went against the barbs and over the palings [pickets] of almost every fence which those who controlled social and political power had erected to restrict our roles in the life of the country" (C, 57).

And as a boy, he and his friends had constructed their heroes from fragments of myth and legend, from the movies ("improvising their rather tawdry and opportunistic version of a national mythology" [AS, 42]), from music and religion, from anything "which violated all ideas of social hierarchy and order" and "which evolved from our wildly improvisatory projections" (C, 58). In a sense this can stand as a model of Ellison's fictive and moral strategy, as of his conception of cultural identity and American pluralism. A complex eclecticism is presented as a moral necessity as much as a natural product of American circumstances. And "complexity" is a favorite word—sometimes "a stubborn complexity." For his is a sensibility that reaches out to absorb the variegated realities of American life, rejecting those who see the process of self-invention as necessitating a denial of that complexity.

The problem is to discover a means of rendering that complexity without reducing it through the sheer process of transmuting experience into art. Pure energy has no shape. The challenge confronting the artist, no less than that confronting the uncodified, free-floating sensibility of the American individual, is to sustain some kind of creative tension between a liberated and liberating imagination and the aesthetic and moral demands of an art and a life which require the subordination of random energy and an anarchic imagination to the constraints of order. For just as the artist operates "within the historical frame of his given art" (AS, 29), so the individual is located within the triangulation of time, space, and cultural inheritance. Thus the writer's responsibility in America is to define the diversity of American experience in such a way as to bring to bear the "unifying force of its vision and its power to give meaningful focus to apparently unrelated emotions and experience" (AS, 31).

The problem is that the democratic ideal of "unity-in-diversity and oneness-in-manyness" (AS, 36) creates a vertigo which he sees as sending too many plunging into the reassurance of simplified cultural models, preferring fragment to complexly formulated whole. There is a clearly positive and negative model of chaos in his mind. On the one hand, there is a fructifying interaction of differing cultural traditions, "always in cacophonic motion. Constantly changing its mode ... a vortex of discordant ways of living and tastes, values and traditions, a whirlpool of odds and ends" (AS, 36) which inspires a profound unease but which is the source of a creative flux. On the other hand, there is a negative chaos, a fearful splintering into component elements. And this is how he saw the black aestheticians of the 1960s. "In many ways," he insisted, "the call for a new social order based upon the glorification of ancestral blood and ethnic background acts as a call to cultural and aesthetic chaos." Yet, "while this latest farcical phase in the drama of American social hierarchy unfolds, the irrepressible movement of American culture toward the integration of its diverse elements continues, confounding the circumlocutions of its staunchest opponents" (AS, 37).

For Ellison, strength lies precisely in diversity, in the sustained tension between chaos and form, the Apollonian and the Dionysian, and this is no less true of a racial identity which he refuses to grant the simple self-evident contours demanded by some of his contemporaries. To his mind, that identity can only express itself multivocally. And so in his essay "The Little Man at Chehaw Station," which is a crucial statement of his artistic and social principles, he recalls seeing a black American who seemed to combine a whole kaleidoscope of cultural influences: and whatever sheerly ethnic identity was communicated by his costume depended upon the observer's ability to see order in an apparent cultural chaos. The essence of the man, his complex identity, existed less in the apparent clashing of styles than in the eclectic imagination, the unabashed assertion of will, which lay behind it—"not in the somewhat comic clashing of styles, but in the mixture, the improvised form, the willful juxtaposition of modes" (AS, 38–39). But, as ever, Ellison is not content to leave it there for, he insists, "his clashing of styles ... sounded an integrative, vernacular note—an American compulsion to improvise upon the given," and the freedom he exercised was "an American freedom" (AS, 39).

It is not hard to see what infuriated the cultural nationalists of the 1960s. Ellison seems to be appropriating supposedly unique and definitional aspects of black life to an American cultural norm. Since America was diverse, loose-limbed, disparate, self-displaying, free-wheeling and concerned with the question of identity, with delineating its own cultural boundaries, with negotiating a relationship with its own past which would give it space for its own critical act of self-invention, the black American was apparently simply an expression of this process, one component of the American diorama. But such an assumption ignored Ellison's central conviction—the basis, indeed, of his whole aesthetic and social theory—namely, that the American identity he described was as it was precisely because of the presence of the Negro. While rigidly subordinating and segregating the black American, the whites had been shaped by what they had tried so hard to exclude. Their imagination had been penetrated, their sensibility infiltrated, by those whose experience of adjusting to a strange land and whose necessary cultural improvisations were more intensely, more deeply scarring, more profoundly disturbing than their own. As the victims of violence, as the evidence of a failure of American idealism, as an extreme case of adjustment to a hostile environment, they represented not merely a constant reminder of the poles of American moral experience but a model of possibility, a paradigm of those acts of desperate self-creation that were at the heart of the American myth. The shadow of the Negro does indeed fall across American history but not merely as promise and threat. His existence defines the nature of the American experience.

Ellison was less inclined than many to abandon the notion of the "melting pot," though he saw the image less as a promise of homogeneity than as a metaphor of "the mystery of American identity (our unity-within-diversity)," and as a symbol of those who "improvised their culture as they did their politics and institutions" (*AS*, 40). The potency of the image lay in its acknowledgment of the fact that, in America, cultural traditions were brought into violent contact, that past and future were made to interact, that ideals, and the evidence of the failure of those ideals, were placed in intimate and ironic counterpoint. And, as a consequence, a series of adjustments were enforced, a process of action and reaction which, to his mind, was the very essence of Americanness. It was precisely on the level of culture that such interactions operated. Cultural appropriation and misappropriation were, to Ellison, the essence of an American development that would scarcely stand still long enough for confident definition. Indeed, since America was to him more a process than an isolable set of characteristics, such definitions carry the threat of a menacing stasis. The essence of improvisation lies in the energy released by the pure act of invention in process. In *Invisible Man* the protagonist is at his most vulnerable when he allows himself to be contained and defined by simple racial or political models. He radiates the energy of pure possibility (like the light bulbs with which he illuminates his darkness) when he abandons these restrictive definitions for the sheer flux of being—a state controlled only by the imagination, and those moral commitments that lead him out of his isolation and into the dangerous interactions of the outside world and the complex symbols of the novel, with which he seeks to address that "variegated audience" for whom the little man at Chehaw Station was Ellison's image. As he himself insists, "it is the very spirit of art to be defiant of categories and obstacles.... They [the images of art or the sound of music] are, as transcendent forms of symbolic expression, agencies of human freedom" (*AS*, 44). For Ellison, "the work of art" itself "is ... an act of faith in our ability to communicate symbolically" (*AS*, 53).

Invisible Man opens and concludes with references to jazz. At the beginning the protagonist sits in his cellar and "feels" rather than listens to the music of Louis Armstrong who has "made poetry out of being invisible."[9] High on drugs, he responds to the off-beats, seeing meaning in the unheard sounds, the resistances to simple rhythmic structure. Music becomes a clue to his past and future. The music pulls him back to his origins, conjuring up an image of his slave past; but it also offers him a clue to his future, outside the determined structures of social life. The music, like the novel the protagonist writes, emerges from "an urge to make music of invisibility," to set it down. It is a paradoxical enterprise. But, then, as we are told at the end of the novel, the music, too, is characterized by "diversity." It, too, contains an essential conflict. And that conflict mirrors the conflict of the protagonist who reminds himself that "the mind that has conceived a plan of living must never lose sight of the chaos against which that pattern was conceived." And this, he assures us, "goes for societies as for individuals" (*IM*, 438). It is the virtue of jazz that its improvisations remind us of precisely this. Improvisation has its risks. In the form of Rinehart, a protean figure (whose first name is actually Proteus) who refuses all content and all commitment, it becomes pure chaos; but for the protagonist, willing, finally, to chance his own dangerous act of self-creation in the public world outside his cellar, it becomes a commitment to sustaining the tension between the twin compulsions of freedom and order.

Jazz operates in Ellison's work as image and fact. The thematic uses he makes of it have been usefully traced by Robert G. O'Meally in *The Craft of Ralph Ellison.* Jazz exists as a constant source of reference, an ironic counterpoint to the protagonist's earnest struggles, a celebration of his growing understanding. Ellison himself has spoken of his desire to capture the "music and idiom" of American Negro speech, but in fact his concern with musical structures goes much further than this. In "A Song of Innocence" the prose owes less to idiomatic speech than to jazz rhythms, the words being of less significance than the free flow of sound. Indeed the inadequacy of language, which is in part the subject of that story, implies the need to turn to other models, other symbols as a means of explaining the conflicting demands of pattern and chaos, form and experience, tradition and innovation. And throughout his career, Ellison turned to the improvisational thrust of jazz for that symbol, finding there a clue to the commitments required of the artist, the race, and the individual concerned with developing their own identities in the face of inherited forms: "I had learned from the jazz musicians I had known as a boy in Oklahoma City something of the discipline and devotion to his art required of the artist ... the give and take, the subtle rhythmical sharpening and blending of idea, tone and imagination demanded of group improvisations" (*S&A*, 189–90). And "after the jazzman has learned the fundamentals of his instrument and the traditional techniques of jazz—the intonations, the mute work, manipulation of timbre, the body of traditional styles—he must 'find himself,' must be reborn, must find, as it were, his soul. All this through achieving that subtle identification between his instrument and his deepest drives which will allow him to express his own unique ideas and his own unique voice. He must achieve, in short, his self-determined identity" (*S&A*, 209). Like Charlie Parker, he is involved in a struggle "against personal chaos" (*S&A*, 227). To Ellison, much the same could be said of the writer in America, as of the individual struggling to make sense of his racial and cultural inheritance while defining a self strong enough to stand against the centripetal pull of the chaos that could manifest itself equally as pure contingency or deceptive consonance.

In an essay titled "Society, Morality, and the Novel," Ellison observed that "the writer has an obsessive need to play with the fires of chaos and to rearrange reality to the patterns of his imagination,"[10] while the novel achieves its "universality" precisely through "accumulating images of reality and arranging them in patterns of universal significance" (LN, 61). Indeed, it seemed to him possible that the novel, as a form, had evolved in order "to deal with man's growing awareness that behind the facade of social organization, manners, customs, myths, rituals, religions of the post-Christian era, lies chaos" (LN, 64). But since we can live neither "in the contemplation of chaos" nor "without awareness of chaos" (LN, 64–65), the novel simultaneously acknowledges and seeks to transcend the fact that "the treasure of possibility is always to be found in the cave of chaos, guarded by the demons of destruction" (LN, 65). The writer's responsibility, in Ellison's eyes, is to improvise a response that denies nothing of the force and power of disorder but will "strengthen man's will to say No to chaos and affirm him in his task of humanizing himself and the world" (LN, 66), without submitting to stasis. Change and diversity are, to him, the essence of the American experience. The challenge is to bring to "the turbulence of change" an "imaginative integration and moral continuity" (LN, 69)—to improvise America, as the individual creates the uncreated features of his face, and as the black American had struggled to "create the consciousness of his oppressed nation."

Notes

1. See Richard Wright, "Blueprint for Negro Literature," *Amistad* 2 (New York, 1971): 11.

2. See Ralph Ellison, "Recent Negro Fiction," *New Masses* 40 (August 5, 1941): 26.

3. "Study and Experience: An Interview with Ralph Ellison," *Massachusetts Review* 18:3 (Autumn 1977): 424. Subsequently cited in text as *MR*.

4. Ralph Ellison, *Shadow and Act* (New York: Random House, 1964), 59. Subsequently cited in text as *S&A*.

5. Ralph Ellison, "The Little Man at Chehaw Station," *American Scholar* 47 (Winter 1977–78): 35. Subsequently cited in text as *AS*.

6. Ralph Ellison, "A Song of Innocence," *Iowa Review* 1 (Spring 1970): 32.

7. Ralph Ellison, "On Initiation Rites and Power: Ralph Ellison Speaks at West Point," *Commentary* 15 (Spring 1974): 186.

8. Ralph Ellison, "On Becoming a Writer," *Commentary* 38 (October 1964): 57. Subsequently cited in text as *C.*

9. Ralph Ellison, *Invisible Man* (New York: Random House, 1952), 8. Subsequently cited in text as *IM.*

10. Ralph Ellison, "Society, Morality, and the Novel," in *The Living Novel: A Symposium*, ed. Granville Hicks (New York: Macmillan, 1957). Subsequently cited in text as *LN.*

IRVING HOWE

Black Boys and Native Sons

James Baldwin first came to the notice of the American literary public not through his own fiction but as author of an impassioned criticism of the conventional Negro novel. In 1949 he published in *Partisan Review* an essay called "Everybody's Protest Novel," attacking the kind of fiction, from *Uncle Tom's Cabin* to *Native Son*, that had been written about the ordeal of the American Negroes; and two years later he printed in the same magazine "Many Thousands Gone," a tougher and more explicit polemic against Richard Wright and the school of naturalistic "protest" fiction that Wright represented. The protest novel, wrote Baldwin, is undertaken out of sympathy for the Negro, but through its need to present him merely as a social victim or a mythic agent of sexual prowess, it hastens to confine the Negro to the very tones of violence he has known all his life. Compulsively re-enacting and magnifying his trauma, the protest novel proves unable to transcend it. So choked with rage has this kind of writing become, it cannot show the Negro as a unique person or locate him as a member of a community with its own traditions and values, its own unspoken recognition of shared experience which creates a way of life." The failure of the protest novel "lies in its insistence that it is [man's] categorization alone which is real and which cannot be transcended."

From *A World More Attractive: A View of Modern Literature and Politics.* © 1963 by Irving Howe. Reprinted by permission.

Like all attacks launched by young writers against their famous elders, Baldwin's essays were also a kind of announcement of his own intentions. He wrote admiringly about Wright's courage ("his work was an immense liberation and revelation for me"), but now, precisely because Wright had prepared the way for all the Negro writers to come, he, Baldwin, would go further, transcending the sterile categories of "Negro-ness," whether those enforced by the white world or those defensively erected by the Negroes themselves. No longer mere victim or rebel, the Negro would stand free in a self-achieved humanity. As Baldwin put it some years later, he hoped "to prevent myself from becoming *merely* a Negro; or even, *merely* a Negro writer." The world "tends to trap and immobilize you in the role you play," and for the Negro writer, if he is to be a writer at all, it hardly matters whether the trap is sprung from motives of hatred or condescension.

Baldwin's rebellion against the older Negro novelist who had served him as a model and had helped launch his career, was not of course an unprecedented event. The history of literature is full of such painful ruptures, and the issue Baldwin raised is one that keeps recurring, usually as an aftermath to a period of "socially engaged" writing. The novel is an inherently ambiguous genre: it strains toward formal autonomy and can seldom avoid being a public gesture. If it is true, as Baldwin said in "Everybody's Protest Novel," that "literature and sociology are not one and the same," it is equally true that such statements hardly begin to cope with the problem of how a writer's own experience affects his desire to represent human affairs in a work of fiction. Baldwin's formula evades, through rhetorical sweep, the genuinely difficult issue of the relationship between social experience and literature.

Yet in *Notes of a Native Son*, the book in which his remark appears, Baldwin could also say: "One writes out of one thing only—one's own experience." What, then, was the experience of a man with a black skin, what *could* it be in this country? How could a Negro put pen to paper, how could he so much as think or breathe, without some impulsion to protest, be it harsh or mild, political or private, released or buried? The "sociology" of his existence formed a constant pressure on his literary work, and not merely in the way this might be true for any writer, but with a pain and ferocity that nothing could remove.

James Baldwin's early essays are superbly eloquent, displaying virtually in full the gifts that would enable him to become one of the great American rhetoricians. But these essays, like some of the later ones, are marred by rifts in logic, so little noticed when one gets swept away by the brilliance of the language that it takes a special effort to attend their argument.

Later Baldwin would see the problems of the Negro writer with a greater charity and more mature doubt. Reviewing in 1959 a book of poems by Langston Hughes, he wrote: "Hughes is an American Negro poet and has no choice but to be acutely aware of it. He is not the first American Negro to find the war between his social and artistic responsibilities all but irreconcilable." All but irreconcilable: the phrase strikes a note sharply different from Baldwin's attack upon Wright in the early fifties. And it is not hard to surmise the reasons for this change. In the intervening years Baldwin had been living through some of the experiences that had goaded Richard Wright into rage and driven him into exile; he too, like Wright, had been to hell and back, many times over.

II

Gawd, Ah wish all them white folks was dead.

The day *Native Son* appeared, American culture was changed forever. No matter how much qualifying the book might later need, it made impossible a repetition of the old lies. In all its crudeness, melodrama and claustrophobia of vision, Richard Wright's novel brought out into the open, as no one ever had before, the hatred, fear and violence that have crippled and may yet destroy our culture.

A blow at the white man, the novel forced him to recognize himself as an oppressor. A blow at the black man, the novel forced him to recognize the cost of his submission. *Native Son* assaulted the most cherished of American vanities: the hope that the accumulated injustice of the past would bring with it no lasting penalties, the fantasy that in his humiliation the Negro somehow retained a sexual potency—or was it a childlike good-nature—that made it necessary to envy and still more to suppress him. Speaking from the black wrath of retribution, Wright insisted that history can be a punishment. He told us the one thing even the most liberal whites preferred not to hear: that Negroes were far from patient or forgiving, that they were scarred by fear, that they hated every moment of their suppression even when seeming most acquiescent, and that often enough they hated *us*, the decent and cultivated white men who from complicity or neglect shared in the responsibility for their plight. If such younger novelists as Baldwin and Ralph Ellison were to move beyond Wright's harsh naturalism and toward more supple modes of fiction, that was possible only because Wright had been there first, courageous enough to release the full weight of his anger.

In *Black Boy*, the autobiographical narrative he published several years later, Wright would tell of an experience he had while working as a bellboy in the South. Many times he had come into a hotel room carrying luggage or food and seen naked white women lounging about, unmoved by shame at his presence, for "blacks were not considered human beings anyway ... I was a non-man ... I felt doubly cast out." With the publication of *Native Son*, however, Wright forced his readers to acknowledge his anger, and in that way, if none other, he wrested for himself a sense of dignity as a man. He forced his readers to confront the disease of our culture, and to one of its most terrifying symptoms he gave the name of Bigger Thomas.

Brutal and brutalized, lost forever to his unexpended hatred and his fear of the world, a numbed and illiterate black boy stumbling into a murder and never, not even at the edge of the electric chair, breaking through to an understanding of either his plight or himself, Bigger Thomas was a part of Richard Wright, a part even of the James Baldwin who stared with horror at Wright's Bigger, unable either to absorb him into his consciousness or eject him from it. Enormous courage, a discipline of self-conquest, was required to conceive Bigger Thomas, for this was no eloquent Negro spokesman, no admirable intellectual or formidable proletarian. Bigger was drawn—one would surmise, deliberately—from white fantasy and white contempt. Bigger was the worst of Negro life accepted, then rendered a trifle conscious and thrown back at those who had made him what he was. "No American Negro exists," Baldwin would later write, "who does not have his private Bigger Thomas living in the skull."

Wright drove his narrative to the very core of American phobia: sexual fright, sexual violation. He understood that the fantasy of rape is a consequence of guilt, what the whites suppose themselves to deserve. He understood that the white man's notion of uncontaminated Negro vitality, little as it had to do with the bitter realities of Negro life, reflected some ill-formed and buried feeling that our culture has run down, lost its blood, become febrile. And he grasped the way in which the sexual issue has been intertwined with social relationships, for even as the white people who hire Bigger as their chauffeur are decent and charitable, even as the girl he accidentally kills is a liberal of sorts, theirs is the power and the privilege. "We black and they white. They got things and we ain't. They do things and we can't."

The novel barely stops to provision a recognizable social world, often contenting itself with cartoon simplicities and yielding almost entirely to the nightmare incomprehension of Bigger Thomas. The mood is apocalyptic, the tone superbly aggressive. Wright was an existentialist long before he heard the name, for he was committed to the literature of extreme situations both through the pressures of his rage and the gasping hope of an ultimate catharsis.

Wright confronts both the violence and the crippling limitations of Bigger Thomas. For Bigger white people are not people at all, but something more, "a sort of great natural force, like a stormy sky looming overhead." And only through violence does he gather a little meaning in life, pitifully little: "he had murdered and created a new life for himself." Beyond that Bigger cannot go.

At first *Native Son* seems still another naturalistic novel: a novel of exposure and accumulation, charting the waste of the undersides of the American city. Behind the book one senses the molding influence of Theodore Dreiser, especially the Dreiser of *An American Tragedy* who knows there are situations so oppressive that only violence can provide their victims with the hope of dignity. Like Dreiser, Wright wished to pummel his readers into awareness; like Dreiser, to overpower them with the sense of society as an enclosing force. Yet the comparison is finally of limited value, and for the disconcerting reason that Dreiser had a white skin and Wright a black one.

The usual naturalistic novel is written with detachment, as if by a scientist surveying a field of operations; it is a novel in which the writer withdraws from a detested world and coldly piles up the evidence for detesting it. *Native Son*, though preserving some of the devices of the naturalistic novel, deviates sharply from its characteristic tone: a tone Wright could not possibly have maintained and which, it may be, no Negro novelist can really hold for long. *Native Son* is a work of assault rather than withdrawal; the author yields himself in part to a vision of nightmare. Bigger's cowering perception of the world becomes the most vivid and authentic component of the book. Naturalism pushed to an extreme turns here into something other than itself, a kind of expressionist outburst, no longer a replica of the familiar social world but a self-contained realm of grotesque emblems.

That *Native Son* has grave faults anyone can see. The language is often coarse, flat in rhythm, syntactically overburdened, heavy with journalistic slag. Apart from Bigger, who seems more a brute energy than a particularized figure, the characters have little reality, the Negroes being mere stock accessories and the whites either "agit-prop" villains or heroic Communists whom Wright finds it easier to admire from a distance than establish from the inside. The long speech by Bigger's radical lawyer Max (again a device apparently borrowed from Dreiser) is ill-related to the book itself: Wright had not achieved Dreiser's capacity for absorbing everything, even the most recalcitrant philosophical passages, into a unified vision of things. Between Wright's feelings as a Negro and his beliefs as a Communist there is hardly a genuine fusion, and it is through this gap that a good part of the novel's unreality pours in.

Yet it should be said that the endlessly-repeated criticism that Wright caps his melodrama with a party-line oration tends to oversimplify the novel, for Wright is too honest simply to allow the propagandistic message to constitute the last word. Indeed, the last word is given not to Max but to Bigger. For at the end Bigger remains at the mercy of his hatred and fear, the lawyer retreats helplessly, the projected union between political consciousness and raw revolt has not been achieved—as if Wright were persuaded that, all ideology apart, there is for each Negro an ultimate trial that he can bear only by himself.

Black Boy, which appeared five years after *Native Son*, is a slighter but more skillful piece of writing. Richard Wright came from a broken home, and as he moved from his helpless mother to a grandmother whose religious fanaticism (she was a Seventh-Day Adventist) proved utterly suffocating, he soon picked up a precocious knowledge of vice and a realistic awareness of social power. This autobiographical memoir, a small classic in the literature of self-discovery, is packed with harsh evocations of Negro adolescence in the South. The young

Wright learns how wounding it is to wear the mask of a grinning niggerboy in order to keep a job. He examines the life of the Negroes and judges it without charity or idyllic compensation—for he already knows, in his heart and his bones, that to be oppressed means to lose out on human possibilities. By the time he is seventeen, preparing to leave for Chicago, where he will work on a WPA project, become a member of the Communist Party, and publish his first book of stories called *Uncle Tom's Children*, Wright has managed to achieve the beginnings of consciousness, through a slow and painful growth from the very bottom of deprivation to the threshold of artistic achievement and a glimpsed idea of freedom.

III

Baldwin's attack upon Wright had partly been anticipated by the more sophisticated American critics. Alfred Kazin, for example, had found in Wright a troubling obsession with violence:

> If he chose to write the story of Bigger Thomas as a grotesque crime story, it is because his own indignation and the sickness of the age combined to make him dependent on violence and shock, to astonish the reader by torrential scenes of cruelty, hunger, rape, murder and flight, and then enlighten him by crude Stalinist homilies.

The last phrase apart, something quite similar could be said about the author of *Crime and Punishment*; it is disconcerting to reflect upon how few novelists, even the very greatest, could pass this kind of moral inspection. For the novel as a genre seems to have an inherent bias toward extreme effects, such as violence, cruelty and the like. More important, Kazin's judgment rests on the assumption that a critic can readily distinguish between the genuine need of a writer to cope with ugly realities and the damaging effect these realities may have upon his moral and psychic life. But in regard to contemporary writers one finds it very hard to distinguish between a valid portrayal of violence and an obsessive involvement with it. A certain amount of obsession may be necessary for the valid portrayal—writers devoted to themes of desperation cannot keep themselves morally intact. And when we come to a writer like Richard Wright, who deals with the most degraded and inarticulate sector of the Negro world, the distinction between objective rendering and subjective immersion becomes still more difficult, perhaps even impossible. For a novelist who has lived through the searing experiences that Wright has there cannot be much possibility of approaching his subject with the "mature" poise recommended by high-minded critics. What is more, the very act of writing his novel, the effort to confront what Bigger Thomas means to him, is for such a writer a way of dredging up and then perhaps shedding the violence that society has pounded into him. Is Bigger an authentic projection of a social reality, or is he a symptom of Wright's "dependence on violence and shock?" Obviously both; and it could not be otherwise.

For the reality pressing upon all of Wright's work was a nightmare of remembrance, everything from which he had pulled himself out, with an effort and at a cost that is almost unimaginable. Without the terror of that nightmare it would have been impossible for Wright to summon the truth of the reality—not the only truth about American Negroes, perhaps not even the deepest one, but a primary and inescapable truth. Both truth and terror rested on a gross fact which Wright alone dared to confront: that violence is a central fact in the life of the American Negro, defining and crippling him with a harshness few other Americans need suffer. "No American Negro exists who does not have his private Bigger Thomas living in the skull."

Now I think it would be well not to judge in the abstract, or with much haste, the violence that gathers in the Negro's heart as a response to the violence he encounters in society. It would be well to see this violence as part of an historical experience that is open to moral scrutiny but ought to be shielded from presumptuous moralizing. Bigger Thomas may be enslaved to a hunger for violence, but anyone reading *Native Son* with mere courtesy must observe the way in which Wright, even while yielding emotionally to Bigger's deprivation, also struggles to transcend it. That he did not fully succeed seems obvious; one may doubt that any Negro writer can.

More subtle and humane than either Kazin's or Baldwin's criticism is a remark made by Isaac Rosenfeld while reviewing *Black Boy*: "As with all Negroes and all men who are born to suffer social injustice, part of [Wright's] humanity found itself only in acquaintance with violence, and in hatred of the oppressor." Surely Rosenfeld was not here inviting an easy acquiescence in violence; he was trying to suggest the historical context, the psychological dynamics, which condition the attitudes all Negro writers take, or must take, toward violence. To say this is not to propose the condescension of exempting Negro writers from moral judgment, but to suggest the terms of understanding, and still more, the terms of hesitation for making a judgment.

There were times when Baldwin grasped this point better than anyone else. If he could speak of the "unrewarding rage" of *Native Son*, he also spoke of the book as "an immense liberation." Is it impudent to suggest that one reason he felt the book to be a liberation was precisely its rage, precisely the relief and pleasure that he, like so many other Negroes, must have felt upon seeing those long-suppressed emotions finally breaking through?

The kind of literary criticism Baldwin wrote was very fashionable in America during the post-war years. Mimicking the Freudian corrosion of motives and bristling with dialectical agility, this criticism approached all ideal claims, especially those made by radical and naturalist writers, with a weary skepticism and proceeded to transfer the values such writers were attacking to the perspective from which they attacked. If Dreiser wrote about the power hunger and dream of success corrupting American society, that was because he was really infatuated with them. If Farrell showed the meanness of life in the Chicago slums, that was because he could not really escape it. If Wright portrayed the violence gripping Negro life, that was because he was really obsessed with it. The word "really" or more sophisticated equivalents could do endless service in behalf of a generation of intellectuals soured on the tradition of protest but suspecting they might be pigmies in comparison to the writers who had protested. In reply, there was no way to "prove" that Dreiser, Farrell and Wright were not contaminated by the false values they attacked; probably, since they were mere mortals living in the present society, they were contaminated; and so one had to keep insisting that such writers were nevertheless presenting actualities of modern experience, not merely phantoms of their neuroses.

If Bigger Thomas, as Baldwin said, "accepted a theology that denies him life," if in his Negro self-hatred he "*wants* to die because he glories in his hatred," this did not constitute a criticism of Wright unless one were prepared to assume what was simply preposterous: that Wright, for all his emotional involvement with Bigger, could not see beyond the limitations of the character he had created. This was a question Baldwin never seriously confronted in his early essays. He would describe accurately the limitations of Bigger Thomas and then, by one of those rhetorical leaps at which he is so gifted, would assume that these were also the limitations of Wright or his book.

Still another ground for Baldwin's attack was his reluctance to accept the clenched militancy of Wright's posture as both novelist and man. In a remarkable sentence appearing in "Everybody's Protest Novel," Baldwin wrote, "our humanity is our burden, our life; we need not battle for it; we need only to do what is infinitely more difficult— that is, accept it." What Baldwin was saying here was part of the outlook so many American intellectuals took over during the years of a post-war liberalism not very different from conservatism. Ralph Ellison expressed this view in terms still more extreme: "Thus to see America with an awareness of its rich diversity and its almost magical fluidity and freedom, I was forced to conceive of a novel unburdened by the narrow naturalism which has led after so many triumphs to the final and unrelieved despair which marks so much of our current fiction." This note of willed affirmation—as if one could *decide* one's deepest and most authentic response to society!—was to be heard in many other works of the early fifties, most notably in Saul Bellow's *Adventures of Augie March*. Today it is likely to strike one as a note whistled in the dark. In response to Baldwin and Ellison, Wright would have said (I virtually quote the words he used in talking to me during the summer of 1958) that only through struggle could men with black skins, and for that matter, all the oppressed of the world, achieve their humanity. It was a lesson, said Wright with a touch of bitterness yet not without kindness, that the younger writers would have to learn in their own way and their own time. All that has happened since, bears him out.

One criticism made by Baldwin in writing about *Native Son*, perhaps because it is the least ideological, remains important. He complained that in Wright's novel "a necessary dimension has been cut away; this dimension being the relationship that Negroes bear to one another, that depth of involvement and unspoken recognition of shared experience which creates a way of life." The climate of the book, "common to most Negro protest novels ... has led us all to believe that in Negro life there exists no tradition, no field of manners, no possibility of ritual or intercourse, such as may, for example, sustain the Jew even after he has left his father's house." It could be urged, perhaps, that in composing a novel verging on expressionism Wright need not be expected to present the Negro world with fullness, balance or nuance; but there can be little doubt that in this respect Baldwin did score a major point: the posture of militancy, no matter how great the need for it, exacts a heavy price from the writer, as indeed from everyone else. For "Even the hatred of squalor / Makes the brow grow stern / Even anger against injustice / Makes the voice grow harsh ..." All one can ask, by way of reply, is whether the refusal to struggle may not exact a still greater price. It is a question that would soon be tormenting James Baldwin, and almost against his will.

IV

In his own novels Baldwin hoped to show the Negro world in its diversity and richness, not as a mere spectre of protest; he wished to show it as a living culture of men and women who, even when deprived, share in the emotions and desires of common humanity. And he meant also to evoke something of the distinctiveness of Negro life in America, as evidence of its worth, moral tenacity and right to self-acceptance. How can one not sympathize with such a program? And how, precisely as one does sympathize, can one avoid the conclusion that in this effort Baldwin has thus far failed to register a major success?

His first novel, *Go Tell It on the Mountain*, is an enticing but minor work: it traces the growing-up of a Negro boy in the atmosphere of a repressive Calvinism, a Christianity stripped of grace and brutal with fantasies of submission and vengeance. No other work of American fiction reveals so graphically the way in which an oppressed minority aggravates its own oppression through the torments of religious fanaticism. The novel is also striking as a modest *Bildungsroman*, the education of an imaginative Negro boy caught in the heart-struggle between his need to revolt, which would probably lead to his destruction in the jungles of New York, and the miserly consolations of black Calvinism, which would signify that he accepts the denial of his personal needs. But it would be a mistake to claim too much for this first novel, in which a rhetorical flair and a conspicuous sincerity often eat away at the integrity of event and the substance of character. The novel is intense, and the intensity is due to Baldwin's absorption in that religion of denial which leads the boy to become a preacher in his father's church, to scream out God's word from "a merciless resolve to kill my father rather than allow my father to kill me." Religion has of course played a central role in Negro life, yet one may doubt that the special kind of religious experience dominating *Go Tell It on the Mountain* is any more representative of that life, any more advantageous a theme for gathering in the qualities of Negro culture, than the violence and outrage of *Native Son*. Like Wright before him, Baldwin wrote from the intolerable pressures of his own experience; there was no alternative; each had to release his own agony before he could regard Negro life with the beginnings of objectivity.

Baldwin's second novel, *Giovanni's Room*, seems to me a flat failure. It abandons Negro life entirely (not in itself a cause for judgment) and focuses upon the distraught personal relations of several young Americans adrift in Paris. The problem of homosexuality, which is to recur in Baldwin's fiction, is confronted with a notable courage, but also with a disconcerting kind of sentimentalism, a quavering and sophisticated submission to the ideology of love. It is one thing to call for the treatment of character as integral and unique; but quite another for a writer with Baldwin's background and passions to succeed in bringing together his sensibility as a Negro and his sense of personal trouble.

Baldwin has not yet managed—the irony is a stringent one—in composing the kind of novel he counterposed to the work of Richard Wright. He has written three essays, ranging in tone from disturbed affection to disturbing malice, in which he tries to break from his rebellious dependency upon Wright, but he remains tied to the memory of the older man. The Negro writer who has come closest to satisfying Baldwin's program is not Baldwin himself but Ralph Ellison, whose novel *Invisible Man* is a brilliant though flawed achievement, standing with *Native Son* as the major fiction thus far composed by American Negroes.

What astonishes one most about *Invisible Man* is the apparent freedom it displays from the ideological and emotional penalties suffered by Negroes in this country—I say "apparent" because the freedom is not quite so complete as the book's admirers like to suppose.

Still, for long stretches *Invisible Man* does escape the formulas of protest, local color, genre quaintness and jazz chatter. No white man could have written it, since no white man could know with such intimacy the life of the Negroes from the inside; yet Ellison writes with an ease and humor which are now and again simply miraculous.

Invisible Man is a record of a Negro's journey through contemporary America, from South to North, province to city, naïve faith to disenchantment and perhaps beyond. There are clear allegorical intentions (Ellison is "literary" to a fault) but with a book so rich in talk and drama it would be a shame to neglect the fascinating surface for the mere depths. The beginning is both nightmare and farce. A timid Negro boy comes to a white smoker in a Southern town: he is to be awarded a scholarship. Together with several other Negro boys he is rushed to the front of the ballroom, where a sumptuous blonde tantalizes and frightens them by dancing in the nude. Blindfolded, the Negro boys stage a "battle royal," a free-for-all in which they pummel each other to the drunken shouts of the whites. Practical jokes, humiliations, terror—and then the boy delivers a prepared speech of gratitude to his white benefactors. At the end of this section, the boy dreams that he has opened the briefcase given him together with his scholarship to a Negro college and that he finds an inscription reading: "To Whom It May Concern: Keep This Nigger-Boy Running."

He keeps running. He goes to his college and is expelled for having innocently taken a white donor through a Negro ginmill which also happens to be a brothel. His whole experience is to follow this pattern. Strip down a pretense, whether by choice or accident, and you will suffer penalties, since the rickety structure of Negro respectability rests upon pretense and those who profit from it cannot bear to have the reality exposed (in this case, that the college is dependent upon the Northern white millionaire). The boy then leaves for New York, where he works in a white-paint factory, becomes a soapboxer for the Harlem Communists, the darling of the fellow-travelling bohemia, and a big wheel in the Negro world. At the end, after witnessing a frenzied race riot in Harlem, he "finds himself" in some not entirely specified way, and his odyssey from submission to autonomy is complete.

Ellison has an abundance of that primary talent without which neither craft nor intelligence can save a novelist: he is richly, wildly inventive; his scenes rise and dip with tension, his people bleed, his language sings. No other writer has captured so much of the bidden gloom and surface gaiety of Negro life.

There is an abundance of superbly-rendered speech: a West Indian woman inciting her men to resist an eviction, a Southern sharecropper calmly describing how he seduced his daughter, a Harlem street-vender spinning jive. The rhythm of Ellison's prose is harsh and nervous, like a beat of harried alertness. The observation is expert: he knows exactly how zootsuiters walk, making stylization their principle of life, and exactly how the antagonism between American and West Indian Negroes works itself out in speech and humor. He can accept his people as they are, in their blindness and hope:—here, finally, the Negro world does exist, seemingly apart from plight or protest. And in the final scene Ellison has created an unforgettable image: "Ras the Destroyer," a Negro nationalist, appears on a horse dressed in the costume of an Abyssinian chieftain, carrying spear and shield, and charging wildly into the police—a black Quixote, mad, absurd, unbearably pathetic.

But even Ellison cannot help being caught up with *the idea* of the Negro. To write simply about "Negro experience" with the esthetic distance urged by the critics of the fifties, is a moral and psychological impossibility, for plight and protest are inseparable from that experience, and even if less political than Wright and less prophetic than Baldwin, Ellison knows this quite as well as they do.

If *Native Son* is marred by the ideological delusions of the 'thirties, *Invisible Man* is marred, less grossly, by those of the 'fifties. The middle section of Ellison's novel, dealing with the Harlem Communists, does not ring quite true, in the way a good portion of the writings on this theme during the post-war years does not ring quite true. Ellison makes his Stalinist figures so vicious and stupid that one cannot understand how they could ever have attracted him or any other Negro. That the party leadership manipulated members with deliberate cynicism is beyond doubt, but this cynicism was surely more complex and guarded than Ellison shows it to be. No party leader would ever tell a prominent Negro Communist, as one of them does in *Invisible Man*: "You were not hired [as a functionary] to think"—even if that were what he felt. Such passages are almost as damaging as the propagandist outbursts in *Native Son*.

Still more troublesome, both as it breaks the coherence of the novel and reveals Ellison's dependence on the post-war *Zeitgeist*, is the sudden, unprepared and implausible assertion of unconditioned freedom with which the novel ends. As the hero abandons the Communist Party he wonders, "Could politics ever be an expression of love?" This question, more portentous than profound, cannot easily be reconciled to a character who has been presented mainly as a passive victim of his experience. Nor is one easily persuaded by the hero's discovery that "my world has become one of infinite possibilities," his refusal to be the "invisible man" whose body is manipulated by various social groups. Though the unqualified assertion of self-liberation was a favorite strategy among American literary people in the 'fifties, it is also vapid and insubstantial. It violates the reality of social life, the interplay between external conditions and personal will, quite as much as the determinism of the 'thirties. The unfortunate fact remains that to define one's individuality is to stumble upon social barriers which stand in the way, all too much in the way, of "infinite possibilities." Freedom can be fought for, but it cannot always be willed or asserted into existence. And it seems hardly an accident that even as Ellison's hero asserts the "infinite possibilities" he makes no attempt to specify them.

Throughout the 'fifties Richard Wright was struggling to find his place in a world he knew to be changing but could not grasp with the assurance he had felt in his earlier years. He had resigned with some bitterness from the Communist Party, though he tried to preserve an independent radical outlook, tinged occasionally with black nationalism. He became absorbed in the politics and literature of the rising African nations, but when visiting them he felt hurt at how great was the distance between an American Negro and an African. He found life in America intolerable, and he spent his last fourteen years in Paris, somewhat friendly with the intellectual group around Jean-Paul Sartre but finally a loner, a man who stood by the pride of his rootlessness. And he kept writing, steadily experimenting, partly, it may be, in response to the younger men who had taken his place in the limelight and partly because he was truly a dedicated writer.

These last years were difficult for Wright, since he neither made a true home in Paris nor kept in imaginative touch with the changing life of the United States. In the early 'fifties he published a very poor novel *The Outsider*, full of existentialist jargon applied but not really absorbed to the Negro theme. He was a writer in limbo, and his better fiction, such as the novelette "The Man Who Lived Underground," is a projection of that state.

In the late 'fifties Wright published another novel, *The Long Dream*, which is set in Mississippi and displays a considerable recovery of his powers. This book has been criticized for presenting Negro life in the South through "old-fashioned" images of violence, but one ought to hesitate before denying the relevance of such images or joining in the criticism of their use. For Wright was perhaps justified in not paying attention to the changes that have occurred in the South these past few decades. When Negro liberals write that despite the prevalence of bias there has been an improvement in the life of their people, such statements are reasonable and necessary. But what have these to do with the way Negroes feel, with the power of the memories they must surely retain? About this we know very little and would be well advised not to nourish preconceptions, for their feelings may be much closer to Wright's rasping outbursts than to the more modulated tones of the younger Negro novelists. *Wright remembered*, and what he remembered other Negroes must also have remembered. And in that way he kept faith with the experience of the boy who had fought his way out of the depths, to speak for those who remained there.

His most interesting fiction after *Native Son* is to be found in a posthumous collection of stories, *Eight Men*, written during the last 25 years of his life. Though they fail to yield any clear line of chronological development, these stories give evidence of Wright's literary restlessness, his often clumsy efforts to break out of the naturalism which was his first and, I think, necessary mode of expression. The unevenness of his writing is highly disturbing: one finds it hard to understand how the same man, from paragraph to paragraph, can be so brilliant and inept. Time after time the narrative texture is broken by a passage of sociological or psychological jargon; perhaps the later Wright tried too hard, read too much, failed to remain sufficiently loyal to the limits of his talent.

Some of the stories, such as "Big Black Good Man," are enlivened by Wright's sardonic humor, the humor of a man who has known and released the full measure of his despair but finds that neither knowledge nor release matters in a world of despair. In "The Man Who Lived Underground," Wright shows a sense of narrative rhythm, which is superior to anything in his full-length novels and evidence of the seriousness with which he kept working.

The main literary problem that troubled Wright in recent years was that of rendering his naturalism a more terse and supple instrument. I think he went astray whenever he abandoned naturalism entirely: there are a few embarrassingly bad experiments with stories employing self-consciously Freudian symbolism. Wright needed the accumulated material of circumstance which naturalistic detail provided his fiction; it was as essential to his ultimate effect of shock and bruise as dialogue to Hemingway's ultimate effect of irony and loss. But Wright was correct in thinking that the problem of detail is the most vexing technical problem the naturalist writer must face, since the accumulation that makes for depth and solidity can also create a pall of tedium. In "The Man Who Lived Underground" Wright came close to solving this problem, for here the naturalistic detail is put at the service of a radical projective image—a Negro trapped in a sewer; and despite some flaws, the story is satisfying both for its tense surface and elasticity of suggestion.

Richard Wright died at 52, full of hopes and projects. Like many of us, he had somewhat lost his intellectual way but he kept struggling toward the perfection of his craft and toward a comprehension of the strange world that in his last years was coming into birth. In the most fundamental sense, however, he had done his work: he had told his contemporaries a truth so bitter, they paid him the tribute of trying to forget it.

V

Looking back to the early essays and fiction of James Baldwin, one wishes to see a little further than they at first invite:—to see past their brilliance of gesture, by which older writers could be dismissed, and past their aura of gravity, by which a generation of intellectuals could be enticed. After this hard and dismal decade, what strikes one most of all is the sheer pathos of these early writings, the way they reveal the desire of a greatly talented young man to escape the scars—and why should he not have wished to escape them?—which he had found upon the faces of his elders and knew to be gratuitous and unlovely.

Chekhov once said that what the aristocratic Russian writers assumed as their birthright, the writers who came from the lower orders had to pay for with their youth. James Baldwin did not want to pay with his youth, as Richard Wright had paid so dearly. He wanted to move, as Wright had not been able to, beyond the burden or bravado of his stigma; he wanted to enter the world of freedom, grace, and self-creation. One would need a heart of stone, or be a brutal moralist, to feel anything but sympathy for this desire. But we do not make our circumstances; we can, at best, try to remake them. And all the recent writing of Baldwin indicates that the wishes of his youth could not be realized, not in *this* country. The sentiments of humanity which had made him rebel against Richard Wright have now driven him back to a position close to Wright's rebellion.

Baldwin's most recent novel *Another Country* is a "protest novel" quite as much as *Native Son*, and anyone vindictive enough to make the effort, could score against it the points Baldwin scored against Wright. No longer is Baldwin's prose so elegant or suave as it was once; in this book it is harsh, clumsy, heavy-breathing with the pant of suppressed bitterness. In about half of *Another Country*—the best half, I would judge—the material is handled in a manner somewhat reminiscent of Wright's naturalism: a piling on of the details of victimization, as the jazz musician Rufus Scott, a sophisticated distant cousin of Bigger Thomas, goes steadily down the path of self-destruction, worn out in the effort to survive in the white man's jungle and consumed by a rage too extreme to articulate yet too amorphous to act upon. The narrative voice is a voice of anger, rasping and thrusting, not at all "literary" in the somewhat lacquered way the earlier Baldwin was able to achieve. And what that voice says, no longer held back by the proprieties of literature, is that the nightmare of the history we have made allows us no immediate escape. Even if all the visible tokens of injustice were erased, the Negroes would retain their hatred and the whites their fear and guilt. Forgiveness cannot be speedily willed, if willed at all, and before it can even be imagined there will have to be a fuller discharge of those violent feelings that have so long been suppressed. It is not a pretty thought, but neither is it a mere "unrewarding rage"; and it has the sad advantage of being true, first as Baldwin embodies it in the disintegration of Rufus, which he portrays with a ferocity quite new in his fiction, and then as he embodies it in the hard-driving ambition of Rufus' sister Ida, who means to climb up to success even if she has to bloody a good many people, whites preferably, in order to do it.

Another Country has within it another novel: a nagging portrayal of that entanglement of personal relationships—sterile, involuted, grindingly rehearsed, pursued with quasi-religious fervor, and cut off from any dense context of social life—which has come to be a standard element in contemporary fiction. The author of *this* novel is caught up with the problem of communication, the emptiness that seeps through the lives of many cultivated persons and in response to which he can only reiterate the saving value of true and lonely love. These portions of *Another Country* tend to be abstract, without the veined milieu, the filled-out world, a novel needs: as if Baldwin, once he moves away from the Negro theme, finds it quite as hard to lay hold of contemporary experience as do most other novelists. The two pulls upon his attention are difficult to reconcile, and Baldwin's future as a novelist is decidedly uncertain.

During the last few years James Baldwin has emerged as a national figure, the leading intellectual spokesman for the Negroes, whose recent essays, as in *The Fire Next Time*, reach heights of passionate exhortation unmatched in modern American writing. Whatever his ultimate success or failure as a novelist, Baldwin has already secured his place as one of the two or three greatest essayists this country has ever produced. He has brought a new luster to the essay as an art form, a form with possibilities for discursive reflection and concrete drama which make it a serious competitor to the novel, until recently almost unchallenged as the dominant literary genre in our time. Apparently drawing upon Baldwin's youthful experience as the son of a Negro preacher, the style of these essays is a remarkable instance of the way in which a grave and sustained eloquence—the rhythm of oratory, but that rhythm held firm and hard—can be employed in an age deeply suspicious of rhetorical prowess. And in pieces like the reports on Harlem and the account of his first visit South, Baldwin realizes far better than in his novel the goal he had set himself of presenting Negro life through an "unspoken recognition of shared experience." Yet it should also be recognized that these essays gain at least some of their resonance from the tone of unrelenting protest in which they are written, from the very anger, even the violence Baldwin had begun by rejecting.

Like Richard Wright before him, Baldwin has discovered that to assert his humanity he must release his rage. But if rage makes for power it does not always encourage clarity, and the truth is that Baldwin's most recent essays are shot through with intellectual confusions, torn by the conflict between his assumption that the Negro must find an honorable place in the life of American society and his apocalyptic sense, mostly fear but just a little hope, that this society is beyond salvation, doomed with the sickness of the West. And again like Wright, he gives way on occasion to the lure of black nationalism. Its formal creed does not interest him, for he knows it to be shoddy, but he is impressed by its capacity to evoke norms of discipline from followers at a time when the Negro community is threatened by a serious inner demoralization.

In his role as spokesman, Baldwin must pronounce with certainty and struggle with militancy; he has at the moment no other choice; yet whatever may have been the objective inadequacy of his polemic against Wright a decade ago, there can be no question but that the refusal he then made of the role of protest reflected faithfully some of his deepest needs and desires. But we do not make our circumstances; we can, at best, try to remake them; and the arena of choice and action always proves to be a little narrower than we had supposed. One generation passes its dilemmas to the next, black boys on to native sons.

"It is in revolt that man goes beyond himself to discover other people, and from this point of view, human solidarity is a philosophical certainty." The words come from Camus: they might easily have been echoed by Richard Wright: and today one can imagine them being repeated, with a kind of rueful passion, by James Baldwin. No more important words could be spoken in our century, but it would be foolish, and impudent, not to recognize that for the men who must live by them the cost is heavy.

Chronology

1914	Birth of Ralph Waldo Ellison on March 1, in Oklahoma City.
1917	Death of Ellison's father, Lewis Ellison.
1920	Attends Frederick Douglass Elementary School.
1929	Hears Lester Young playing with members of the Blue Devils Orchestra—predecessor of Count Basie's Band.
1933	Leaves Oklahoma City for Tuskegee Institute in Alabama.
1936	Moves to New York City to study sculpture and raise money to return to school.
1937	Death of his mother in Dayton, Ohio; spends winter there; returns to New York; first book review published in *New Challenge*.
1938	Joins Federal Writers' Project.
1939	Publishes first short story, "Slick Gonna Learn."
1942	Tries unsuccessfully to enlist in Navy Band; becomes managing editor of *The Negro Quarterly*.
1943	Covers Harlem race riot for *New York Post*; joins Merchant Marine.
1944	Receives Rosenwald Foundation grant.

1945	During summer begins writing *Invisible Man*.
1946	Marries Fanny McConnell.
1952	*Invisible Man* is published.
1953	*Invisible Man* wins the National Book Award.
1955–1957	Lives in Rome.
1958–1961	Instructor in Russian and American literature at Bard College.
1960	London-based literary magazine *Noble Savage* publishes "And Hickman Arrives."
1962–1964	Teaches at Rutgers University.
1964	Random House publishes *Shadow and Act*.
1965	*Invisible Man* selected as most distinguished post-World War II novel in a *Book Week* poll.
1967	Fire in summer home destroys the manuscript of second novel.
1969	Awarded the Medal of Freedom, America's highest civilian honor, by President Lyndon Johnson.
1970	Awarded the *Chevalier de l'Ordre des Artes et Lettres* by André Malraux, the French minister of cultural affairs.
1970–1980	Albert Schweitzer Professor of Humanities at New York University.
1975	Speaks at the opening of the Ralph Ellison Public Library in Oklahoma City.
1982	Random House publishes special Thirtieth Anniversary Edition of *Invisible Man*.
1986	Random House publishes *Going to the Territory*.
1994	Ralph Ellison dies on April 16 at the age of 80 in Harlem.

Works by Ralph Ellison

Invisible Man, 1952.

Shadow and Act, 1964.

Going to the Territory, 1986.

The Collected Essays, 1995.

Flying Home and Other Stories, 1996.

Juneteenth, 1999.

Works about Ralph Ellison

Baumbach, Jonathan. *The Landscape of Nightmare*. New York: New York University Press, 1965.

Blake, Susan. "Ritual and Rationalization: Black Folklore in the Works of Ralph Ellison." *PMLA* 94, no. 1 (January 1979): 121–36.

Bloom, Harold, ed. *Modern Critical Views: Ralph Ellison*. New York: Chelsea House, 1986.

Bone, Robert. "Ralph Ellison and the Uses of Imagination." *Anger and Beyond*. ed. Herbert Hill. New York: Harper & Row, 1966. 86–111.

Busby, Mark. *Ralph Ellison*. Boston: Twayne Publishers, 1991.

Butler, Robert J. "Dante's *Inferno* and Ellison's *Invisible Man*: A Study in Literary Continuity." *CLA Journal* 28 (1984): 57–77.

Callahan, John F. "Chaos, Complexity and Possibility: The Historical Frequencies of Ralph Waldo Ellison." *Black American Literature Forum*. Volume 11, Issue 4 (Winter 1977), 130–38.

Cook, William W. "Ellison's Modern Odysseus." *Humanities* 13:3 (May/June 1992): 26–28.

Cooke, Michael G. *Afro-American Literature in the Twentieth Century: The Achievement of Intimacy*. New Haven: Yale University Press, 1984.

Ellison, Ralph. *Invisible Man*. New York: Vintage Books, 1952, 1982.

———. *Flying Home and Other Stories*. Ed. John Callahan. New York: Random House, 1996.

———. *Going to the Territory*. New York: Random House, 1986.

———. *Juneteenth*. Ed. John Callahan. New York: Random House, 1999.

————. *Shadow and Act*. New York: Random House, 1964.

Goede, William. "On Lower Frequencies: The Buried Men in Wright and Ellison." *Modern Fiction Studies* 15 (1969): 483–501.

Harper, Phillip Brian. *Framing the Margins: The Social Logic of Postmodern Culture*. Oxford: Oxford University Press, 1994.

Hassan, Ihab. *Radical Innocence: Studies in the Contemporary American Novel*. Princeton: Princeton University Press, 1961.

Hersey, John, ed. *Ralph Ellison: A Collection of Critical Essays*. Englewood Cliffs, NJ: Prentice Hall, 1970.

Howe, Irving. *A World More Attractive*. New York: Horizon, 1963.

Kostelanetz, Richard. *Politics in the African-American Novel: James Weldon Johnson, W.E.B. Du Bois, Richard Wright, and Ralph Ellison*. New York: Greenwood Press, 1991.

Lane, James B. "Underground to Manhood: Ralph Ellison's *Invisible Man*." *Negro American Literature Forum*. Volume 7, Issue 2 (Summer, 1973): 64–72.

Lee, Kun Jong. "Ellison's Racial Variations on American Themes." *African American Review*. Volume 30, Issue 3 (Autumn, 1996): 421–440.

Lewis, R.W.B. "The Ceremonial Imagination of Ralph Ellison." *Carleton Miscellany* 18 (1980): 34–38.

————. *Trials of the Word*. New Haven: Yale University Press, 1965.

Lieber, Todd M. "Ralph Ellison and the Metaphor of Invisibility in Black Literary Tradition." *American Quarterly* 24 (1972): 86–100.

McSweeney, Kerry. "*Invisible Man*": *A Student's Companion to the Novel*. Boston: Twayne, 1988.

Nadel, Alan. *Invisible Criticism: Ralph Ellison and the American Canon*. Iowa City: University of Iowa Press, 1988.

Naison, Mark. *Communists in Harlem During the Depression*. Urbana: University of Illinois Press, 1983.

O'Meally, Robert. *The Craft of Ralph Ellison*. Cambridge: Harvard University Press, 1980.

————. *New Essays on "Invisible Man."* New York: Cambridge University Press, 1988.

Reilly, John M., ed. *Twentieth Century Interpretations of Invisible Man*. Englewood Cliffs, NJ: Prentice Hall, 1970.

Rodnon, Stewart. "*The Adventures of Huckleberry Finn* and *Invisible Man*: Thematic and Structural Comparisons." *Negro American Literature Forum* 4 (1970): 45–51.

Rovit, Earl H. "Ralph Ellison and the American Comic Tradition."
     Twentieth Century Interpretations of Invisible Man. ed. John M.
     Reilly. Englewood Cliffs, NJ: Prentice Hall, 1970.
Saunders, Archie D. "Odysseus in Black: An Analysis of the Structure
     of *Invisible Man*." *CLA Journal* 13 (March 1970): 217–28.
Schor, Edith. *Visible Ellison: A Study of Ralph Ellison's Fiction*. Westport,
     CT.: Greenwood Press, 1993.
Skerrett, Joseph T. "The Wright Interpretation: Ralph Ellison and the
     Anxiety of Influence." *Massachusetts Review* 21 (1980): 196–212.
Stepto, Robert B. *From Behind the Veil: A Study of Afro-American
     Narrative*. Urbana: University of Illinois Press, 1979.
Tanner, Tony. *City of Words: American Fiction 1950–1970*. New York:
     Harper and Row, 1971.
Walsh, Mary Ellen Williams. "*Invisible Man*: Ralph Ellison's Waste
     Land." *CLA Journal* 28 (1984): 150–58.
Watts, Jerry Gafio. *Heroism and the Black Intellectual: Ralph Ellison,
     Politics, and Afro-American Intellectual Life*. Chapel Hill: University
     of North Carolina Press, 1994.
West, Anthony. "Black Man's Burden." *Twentieth Century Interpretations
     of Invisible Man*. ed. John M. Reilly. Englewood Cliffs, NJ:
     Prentice Hall, 1970.

WEBSITES

American Masters—Ralph Ellison
http://www.pbs.org/wnet/americanmasters/database/ellison_r_homepage.html

Ralph Ellison's *Invisible Man*
http://www.english.upenn.edu/~afilreis/50s/ellison-main.html

Ralph Ellison Webliography
http://www.centerx.gseis.ucla.edu/weblio/ellison.html

The San Antonio College Litweb Ralph Ellison Page
http://www.accd.edu/sac/english/bailey/ellisonr.htm

Contributors

HAROLD BLOOM is Sterling Professor of the Humanities at Yale University and Henry W. and Albert A. Berg Professor of English at the New York University Graduate School. He is the author of over 20 books, including *Shelley's Mythmaking* (1959), *The Visionary Company* (1961), *Blake's Apocalypse* (1963), *Yeats* (1970), *A Map of Misreading* (1975), *Kabbalah and Criticism* (1975), *Agon: Toward a Theory of Revisionism* (1982), *The American Religion* (1992), *The Western Canon* (1994), and *Omens of Millennium: The Gnosis of Angels, Dreams, and Resurrection* (1996). *The Anxiety of Influence* (1973) sets forth Professor Bloom's provocative theory of the literary relationships between the great writers and their predecessors. His most recent books include *Shakespeare: The Invention of the Human* (1998), a 1998 National Book Award finalist, *How to Read and Why* (2000), and *Genius: A Mosaic of One Hundred Exemplary Creative Minds* (2002). In 1999, Professor Bloom received the prestigious American Academy of Arts and Letters Gold Medal for Criticism, and in 2002 he received the Catalonia International Prize.

NORMA JEAN LUTZ has been writing professionally since 1977. She is the author of more than 250 short stories and articles as well as 40-plus books—fiction and nonfiction.

THOMAS HEISE is a poet and a PhD candidate in English Literature at New York University. His poetry has appeared in *Indiana Review*, *Columbia: A Journal of Literature and Art*, *Southern Humanities Review*, and *The New York Quarterly*.

JOHN M. REILLY is the editor of *Twentieth Century Interpretations of* Invisible Man and is a contributor to *Approaches to Teaching* Invisible Man and *Speaking for You: The Vision of Ralph Ellison*.

C. W. E BIGSBY is Professor of American Studies at the University of East Anglia, Norwich. He has published extensively on aspects of English and American Culture, including *The Second Black Renaissance*, *A Critical Introduction to 20th Century American Drama*, and *The Cambridge Companion to Arthur Miller*.

IRVING HOWE was considered one of America's most influential literary critics at the time of his death in 1993. He was the founding editor of *Dissent* and Distinguished Professor of Literature at City University of New York. Professor Howe's many books include *Beyond the New Left*, *A Margin of Hope: An Intellectual Autobiography*, *Politics and the Novel*, and *A World More Attractive: A View of Modern Literature and Politics*.

INDEX

139